IMAGES OF ENGLAND

BURNLEY INNS
AND TAVERNS

The "OLD BLUE BELL"
BURNLEY

IMAGES OF ENGLAND

BURNLEY INNS AND TAVERNS

JACK NADIN

TEMPUS

Frontispiece: The old Blue Bell, Burnley: the seated couple are thought to have been the landlord and his wife. (Towneley Hall Art Gallery and Museum)

First published 2007

Tempus Publishing Limited
Cirencester Road, Chalford,
Stroud, Gloucestershire, GL6 8PE
www.tempus-publishing.com

British Library Cataloguing in Publication Data.
A catalogue record for this book is available from the British Library.

ISBN 978 0 7524 4413 0

Typesetting and origination by Tempus Publishing Limited.
Printed in Great Britain.

Contents

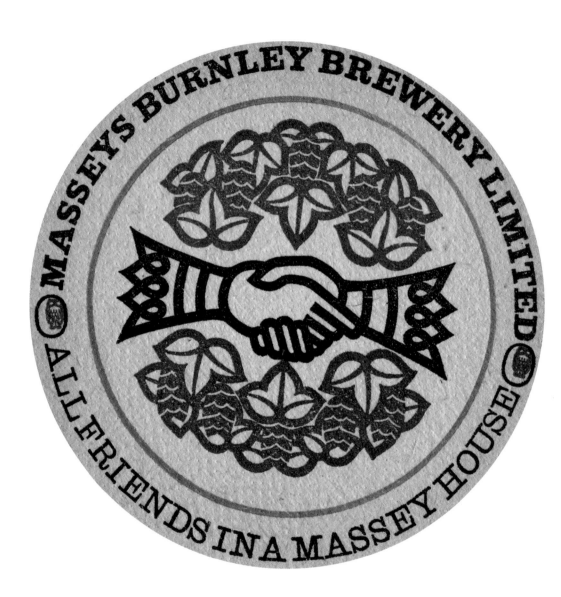

MASSEYS BURNLEY BREWERY LIMITED

ALL FRIENDS IN A MASSEY HOUSE

Introduction

The research and history of local inns and taverns make a fascinating study. The names of the inns themselves can offer clues of places long gone from our local landscape or perhaps give us an indication as to just when the inns were built. Many local pubs have now disappeared from our town, including a great number in and around the town centre and Padiham Road etc, as the town saw a need to move into the future. These are sadly missed, even now, years later by former regulars. The sing-along days with the piano and the 'happy hours' (even before 'happy hours' were invented by modern pubs) still live in the memories of many. Older Burnley residents remember Sunday dinnertimes spent in the local with a game of dominoes, cards or darts, all in friendly company and accompanied by good beer. Pleasant courtship and marriage often arose from a sweet glance in the local pub. I hope that at least some memories of those days now gone will be revived in looking back at Burnley's old inns and taverns. The book is not, I stress, a complete list of Burnley's pubs, although almost three hundred inns are mentioned. Recalled are inns and hotels that some readers will remember. Others are just beyond living memory but recalled in this book all the same, for they did exist. Scant information is available on many beerhouses that used to exist in the town. Beerhouses, where only beer was allowed to be served, were, at one time, on almost every street corner; little wonder Burnley in 1881 was noted as being 'the most drunken town in England'. I have also tried to include, where known, the dates when the pubs closed down, along with other bits of information that make pub debates all the more interesting. Also, snippets from newspapers of the day reporting some of the very strange cases that have occurred in Burnley's pubs in the past have been added for further interest. The inns and taverns marked thus ★ were originally beerhouses.

Jack Nadin, 2007

MASSEY'S

RECOMMENDED
Price list

DRAUGHT BEERS	VAULTS & TAP ROOMS	OTHER ROOMS
Mild (per pint)	1/6	1/7
Bitter (per pint)	1/9	1/10

BOTTLED BEERS & STOUT	ALL ROOMS
Light Ale	1/3
King's Ale	1/7½
Pale Ale	1/5½
Guinness	1/8
Mackeson	1/8½
Bass & Worthington	1/7½
Carlsberg Lager	1/7½
Carling Lager	1/7
Double Diamond	1/7

WINES AND SPIRITS	
Whisky 5 out optic	2/8
Rum „	2/8
Gin „	2/8
(Cordial Extra)	3d
Brandy	3/5
Gin and Vermouth	3/6
Liqueurs	3/3
Advocaat	3/3
Egg Flip	1/10
Port – Fine Old	1/10
Sherry – Fine Golden	1/10
Sherry – Old Brown	1/10
Sherry – Amontillado	2/1
Sherry – Jerez Cream	2/4
Sherry – Tio Pepe	2/4
Sherry – Bristol Cream	2/10
Mineral Waters	9d

Acknowledgments

Most of the photos in this book are from private collections. I would like to take this opportunity of thanking those who contributed photographs for inclusion. These individuals include: Mike Townsend, Towneley Art Gallery and Museums, Roger Frost and the Briercliffe Society. I would also like to thank the staff at Burnley Reference Library for their time in pointing out sources of reference. Local historian Ken Spencer, who, as always, is there when you need him and is invariably there to help in spite of what he might be doing himself. To Tempus Publishing for making this book possible. Lastly, but not least, my wife Rita, who has suffered so much with her illness in recent times, but has always supported my writing of local history. A big thank you to you all; without you and your help this book would not have been possible.

Opposite: A price list from the days when a pint of bitter only cost 1s 9d.

Adelphi Hotel, Railway Street, closed 1997

This once-popular public house is situated on Railway Street, convenient to the Bank Top or Central station, as it is known as today. The inn dates from around 1865, when William Veevers is listed in the directories as landlord, and was obviously built to accommodate railway passengers. In the late 1880s, J. Hargreaves and Sons, of the Old Brewery, who owned or leased another twenty-four pubs in town, owned the pub. There was a remarkable incident on 29 October 1930, when Mrs Florence Hosie had a narrow escape. The first of several coal wagons crashed through the buffers at the Central railway station sidings and went straight through the gable end of the Adelphi pub, demolishing the washhouse and part of its cellar.

At one time, in the not-too-distant past, one of the landlords at the Adelphi kept flesh-eating fish. It was a great delight to purchase a meat pie and drop pieces of crust or meat into the tank and watch the ripples. No one took up the challenge to remove any of the crusts from the tank. In more recent times, around the early 1960s, the landlord at the Adelphi was H. Doney.

This passage was printed in the *Burnley Advertiser*, 3 October 1863:

> Thomas Whittaker of the Adelphi Tap was summoned for assault on Mary Duerden, the wife of John Duerden on Monday night the 21st inst. It appeared that on the night named, the complainant went into the tap with her husband, who left the tap with her. She afterwards missed her husband, and went back to the tap, insisting that he had returned, and abusing the tap-keeper, who got hold of her to drag her into the house so that she might look through it for her husband. He had not returned to the tap. The complainant alleged that Whittaker struck her when dragging her into the house, and knocked the child out of her arms. Complainant called a witness named Edmondson who said he saw the defendant strike her after the child had fallen. The defendant wanted her to go away. When she got home she found her husband there. Two witnesses were called for the defendant. One of them stated that he heard the complainant abusing Whittaker – he did not see the defendant strike. He tried to drag her into the house to search for her husband. She let the child fall out of her arms. Mrs Kidd, who picked up the child, said she let it fall. The case was dismissed.

Albion Inn, 20/22 Red Lion Street, closed 1939

This inn stood at the corner of Croft Street and Red Lion Street – a site now occupied by a greeting-card shop, the address being 20 and 22 Red Lion Street. The pub appears to have dated from 1865, when John Jennings is listed as the landlord there. George Colley was landlord from 1875 to 1887. George lived at the inn with his Irish-born wife Sarah and their son Harry. Job Dean was the longest-serving host from 1890 through to 1914. Nancy Rushton kept the pub in 1923 and George Romney in 1937. The place was also an early meeting house of the local joiners and carpenters union. When the Albion closed, its license was transferred to the 'New Albion' on Rossendale Road, which opened in 1939, hence the name. However, the latter pub is now a restaurant.

The Alma Inn, Accrington Road, named after a battle in the Crimean war.

Alma Inn, 235 Accrington Road

This inn still stands at 235 Accrington Road and its name has obvious connections with the Crimean War. Many Burnley inns and taverns were named after such conflicts, with references to locations of battles and men of war. This battle took place on 20 September 1854, with a loss of 9,000 men – 6,000 of them Russian. The inn probably dates from this time. One incident at the Alma is recorded in the *Burnley Advertiser*, 15 April 1865:

> Henry Schofield was charged with assaulting Alice Astley, who resides with her stepmother at the Alma Inn, Wood Top. The complainant stated that on Monday evening last, the defendant for whom Mr Hartley appeared, went into the house about 8.30. During the night, he began to abuse her mother, whose part she took, saying that if he did not stop she would strike him. He continued to pull the mother about, and then she struck him two or three times. He then turned to her and got hold of her. In the struggle they fell down some steps at the back door, she was down and he struck her and got hold of her by the throat, and injured her so that she could not swallow food in the morning. It appeared from cross-examination by Mr Hartley, that the complainant had been a sweetheart of the defendant, but she declared that she did not want anything more to do with him. A witness named John Hacking, and the stepmother

corroborated the statement of the complainant. The last witness said that she had been much annoyed by the defendant in the house, and all she wanted to do was to prevent him annoying her. He was ordered to enter into his own bond of £50 to keep the peace for six months.

Robert Hargreaves was the landlord in 1868. At one time during the latter part of the nineteenth century, the Alma was owned by William Astley, a Nelson brewer, with as many as twenty premises in town. In 1896, the landlord was John Hartley. In later years, the house became one of the many 'Massey' houses in town. Older regulars may recall James T. Pickup; he kept the pub from around 1937 to about 1953.

Angel Inn, 80 Accrington Road

The Angel Inn at No. 80 Accrington Road is an old Burnley pub dating back to around 1845, and one of the few to retain its original exterior. From a directory we know that Jacob Nowell was the landlord in 1848. There was an interesting and amusing tale told with a mention of the pub back in September 1846, concerning the navvies that were building the railway line just beyond the inn. This was reported in the *Blackburn Standard* on 16 September:

> On Saturday and Sunday last, considerable excitement prevailed in Burnley in consequence of some of the over-lookers or 'gaffers' on the East Lancashire Railway having defrauded their workpeople of their wages. It appears that, on Saturday afternoon, the 'gaffers' received the amount of wages from Mr Hattersley the contractor, and sent it away with their wives intending to follow at an early convenience. The navvies however smelt a rat, and securing the delinquents, kept guard over them in the Angel Inn during Saturday and Sunday. In consequence of the crowd of persons attracted to the place on Sunday, the navvies determined to have an exhibition, and parties were admitted inside the room to 'see the wild beasts', at a charges of a halfpenny each, except 'when feeding', when the charge was a penny. The police however soon interfered, and the prisoners were removed to the Courthouse after offering some considerable resistance. On Monday they were brought before the magistrates, but were dismissed on the grounds that the 'single debts' were too small for magisterial interference, and could only be obtained through the Court of Requests.

The inn was up for sale by auction, as publicised in the *Burnley Advertiser*, 13 November 1858:

> Sale by auction, valuable public house, dwelling houses, cottages, smithy and building land in Habergham Eves, near Burnley. To be sold by auction by William Salisbury at the house of Mr W. Stevenson, the Angel Inn near the barracks in Habergham Eves in the County of Lancaster on Thursday, 26th day of November 1858 at six o'clock in the evening precisely, subject to the conditions then produced, and in the following or such other lots as may be agreed upon at the time of the sale. Lot 1: A Messuage or public house near the barracks in Habergham Eves aforesaid called 'The Angel Inn' fronting the highway leading from Accrington to Burnley, and from Burnley to Padiham, and No. 42 Trinity Street with stables, backyards, and other conveniences thereto belonging and now in the occupation of the said William Stevenson.
> Also two dwelling houses adjoining the said public house on the south easterly side thereof and numbered 2 and 4 in Alma Place in Habergham Eves occupied by Sarah Ann Furness and Mary Taylor.

The landlord, William Stevenson, is mentioned in a court case which took place in 1865. This account is taken from the *Burnley Advertiser*, 1 April 1865:

William Stevenson was summoned for a breach of the Licensed Victualler Act in keeping a disorderly house. Mr Hartley appeared for the defendant. PC O'Gorman said that about two o'clock on the morning of the 16th inst, he was near the Angel Inn when he saw the defendant coming out with only a red petticoat on, and a flannel shirt. He asked the defendant what he was doing out then, and in that state, and he replied that he was only going for a man. Witness then went into the house and in a room there saw two women – a white one and a black one in a nude state. The white woman had red stockings on. The housekeeper was there with a lighted candle, which she blew out as soon as she saw the witness, who then turned on his lamp. There was an old man, a farmer out of the forest as he was told, sitting on a form in a room. The old man was drunk, and the landlord was sharp fresh. Ann Booth the housekeeper was called for the defence. She stated that those in the house went to bed about 11.30. Of the two women, one was a paid servant, and the other was a lodger. These two came downstairs again after going to bed. She heard the noise below and awoke the defendant who had gone to bed intoxicated. He went downstairs, having on his two shirts, one a flannel nightdress he put on when he had to get up at night, and in this state he went out to call a man to help him to get quit of the girls and the old man. When the witness went to bed, she left the cellar door open, and the women had helped themselves. The two women had been discharged the day after, the constable stated that the black woman was there on the 22nd of the month – that the house had been visited at half past eleven at night, and that the old man had been there all night. The witness Booth was recalled once or twice by the Bench, and after a long hearing the defendant was fined 5s and costs. Mr Hartley gave notice of the intention to appeal against the decision of the Bench.

Thwaites' Brewery owned the inn back in 1888 (as they do now) when it held a publican's license, as opposed to being a simple beerhouse, and its rateable value was £71 10d. Inns that held a publican's license were generally more accommodating, comfortable and allowed to sell spirits as well as beer. Today the Angel is a comfortable hostelry, following a recent major refurbishment. Before leaving the Angel, notice the old foot-scraper, or the remains of it, low down on the right-hand side of the front door. This is a reminder of the state of the road that used to run up Sandygate in days of yore. The customers would obligingly wipe the mud off their feet on this before entering the inn. The inn sign today depicts what appears to be an archangel, one of the highest ranks of angels, perhaps reflecting its recent change from an ancient wayside inn to a modern public house!

The Angel features in the *Burnley Gazette*, 19 October 1872:

William Stancliffe, landlord of the Angel Inn, summoned Richard Pilling and Hezekiah Walsh for refusing to quit his house when requested to do so. Mr Baldwin appeared for Stancliffe. Complainant stated that on Thursday, the 3rd inst, defendants were in his house fighting, and when he requested them to leave, they refused. PC Wilkinson gave evidence against Pilling. Fined 5s and costs or seven days. The Mayor said the defendants were liable to a penalty of £5 for this offence. Mr Baldwin said what the defendants were doing would have subjected the landlord to a penalty on the first offence of £10 and £20 on the second offence. It was intimidated that this was the first offence under the new Act, and therefore the defendants were treated leniently.

The modern Baltic Fleet pub of today dates from 1895.

Baltic Fleet*, Briercliffe Road

The Baltic Fleet was originally a beerhouse, dating from the late 1870s when it was run by the Pate family. The premises were in the middle, being one of four cottages. Curiously, it postdates the Battle of the Baltic that took place on 2 April 1801 by over seventy years. The inn sign of today shows the old steam tram, and there are references that the inn was named after these – the local name for these steam and smoke-belching beasts was the 'Baltic Fleet'. Certainly the old trams stopped here before reversing and moving on back to Burnley. However, further conflict arises from the fact that the steam trams were not brought into use until 1881, and we know that Robert Pate was running the beerhouse of that name in 1879. The present premises were built in 1895, as indicated by the datestone above the fine frontage. In the late 1880s, T. Hirst privately owned the inn, though the landlord was James Pilling and the pub was tied to Massey's ales. The house became a 'Massey' house in its own right, probably around the turn of the century.

Before rebuilding, the frontage of the Baltic Fleet had a sunken garden, which was often affected by floodwater until it was levelled off some time afterwards. (Towneley Art Gallery and Museum)

Bank Top Inn*, 2 Parker Street, closed 1936

The license for this beerhouse lapsed in 1936, when £1,665 was paid out in compensation. The Bank Top Inn was another pub owned by William Astley of the Nelson Brewery in 1888. In 1868. the beerhouse was still unnamed, though Patrick Malone was listed as the proprietor. Other landlords here have included John Smith, 1879-1896, although his father Thomas was listed as the head of household in the 1881 census returns. One brawl is described in the *Burnley Gazette*, 3 February 1872:

> Two young men, turners by trade, named respectively Thomas Hitchon and Samuel Barrett, were placed in the dock to answer a charge of assault preferred against them by PC Charles. It appeared that the prisoners, along with two others, had been drinking on Monday afternoon in the Bank Top Inn, Mill Lane, and about four o'clock in the afternoon they all came into the street and commenced to fight. The constable interfered, and tried to separate them, when the two prisoners turned round, knocked him down, and kicked him and struck him with their fists. They afterwards ran away, but were apprehended the same evening. The constable was badly injured about the legs. A witness named Josiah Bradbury deposed to having seen the assault. Defendants denied having committed the assault. The Bench, however, thought the case fully proved, and fined the defendants 40s and costs, or in default one month's imprisonment. Defendants went to prison. Barrett has been previously convicted for assaulting the police.

The women in Burnley also got drunk and aggressive, as reported in the *Burnley Express* on the 21 January 1882:

Her twenty-fifth appearance. Ann Gleeson again appeared in the dock, charged with being drunk. PC 133 stated that on the previous day he saw the prisoner drunk in St James's Street. She was cursing and swearing, and there was a large crowd assembled around her in the street. Between six and nine o'clock he put her out of several public houses and shops and tried to get her to go home. But it was all no use; she was 'a perfect nuisance'. Inspector Procter said he had seen many disgraceful proceedings on the part of women, but he had never seen anything so disgraceful as the conduct of the prisoner when taken into custody. Prisoner: 'I have only just come out of the workhouse your worships'. Mr Briggs: 'I thought you were becoming a reformed character'. The Mayor said that there was a column and a half against the prisoner in the books. The magistrates had been very anxious from time to time to reform her, if possible, but they could not continue any longer, and the prisoner would now be fined 10 shillings and costs, or be sent to gaol for fourteen days with hard labour. Prisoner: 'Thank you, your worships'. (Laughter)

Bankhouse Inn*, 29 Bankhouse Street, closed in 1917

The license for this beerhouse expired in 1917, when £2,500 was paid in compensation. The Bankhouse Inn was situated above Standish Street on the left-hand side going towards Bank Parade, before all this area was demolished. Richard Moore kept the beerhouse from around 1879 to 1893. Richard kept the beerhouse with his wife Nancy, who also looked after the couple's two young children, William and Margaret.

Barracks Tavern, 64 Padiham Road, closed in 1978

The pub took its name from the Burnley Barracks, a military depot dating from 1819. The pub's unofficial name of the 'Museum' was taken from the landlord of the Princess Alexandra in Colne Road who exhibited 'a museum of rare preserved birds, animals, etc., a stereoscopic gallery, a self-acting organ, canaries and walking sticks'. Later in 1870, the same house added a music hall to which 'boys and disorderly persons' were not admitted. The museum transferred to the Barracks Hotel when the landlord, Hezekiah Mitchell, moved there around 1872. In the census returns for that year, we are able to gather more information. Hezekiah was living there with his wife, Mary Ann, and their three children: Sarah, Arthur and Charles. Next came a wonderful array of boarders or lodgers, including John Henry, a comedian, Alice Saul, a pianist, Annie Remrose, a vocalist and George Brown, a pianist and vocalist. Also, there was Henry Holgate, his wife and seven others. The name 'Museum' stuck until the place was demolished to make way for the motorway, along with a greater part of old Whittlefield. The Barracks Tavern was an old building dating from at least 1834, when John Cook is listed as running the inn. The Mitchells held a remarkable record at the 'Museum' and kept the place from 1872, when Hezekiah moved from the Princess Alexandra, through to 1914, when Alfred Mitchell kept the inn. The Barracks Tavern was one of only around six Thwaites' houses in Burnley. The Tavern is mentioned in the *Burnley Advertiser*, 7 January 1865:

> On Monday night last, Mr Daniel Arrowsmith, tailor, gave the men in his employ, about eighteen in number, a supper at the house of Mr James Sutcliffe, Barracks Tavern Inn. After doing justice to the good things provided, the cloth was withdrawn, and Mr D. Healey elected to the chair. The rest of the evening was spent in singing, dancing, reciting and other modes of enjoyment.

Bay Horse Hotel, 58 St James's Street, closed in 1958

The surrender of this license, along with that of the Masons Arms and the Well Hall, was due to the building of the new Keirby Hotel. The Bay Horse Hotel was largely rebuilt in 1894, although the inn dates from at least 1792. In the year 1824, Ellen Whitaker is listed in the directories; she ran the pub until around 1834. John Eastwood was the landlord here in 1864 and mentioned in connection with a court case that year in the *Burnley Advertiser*, 22 October 1864:

> Breach of the Licensed Victualler Act. John Eastwood of the Bay Horse Inn was summoned for a breach of this act by the keeper of his tap. PS Bibby said that on Sunday the 9th inst. he visited the tap at 4.30 in the afternoon. He found three men in, having three glasses on the table before them containing ale. The tap-keeper said one of them was a Burnley man; the other two came from Colne. Mr Eastwood said he was sorry for what had taken place; he was away from home at the time, and he would take care that such a thing did not happen again. The police officer said the tap-keeper was a very respectable man, and kept the tap in a respectable manner. Fined 5s and costs.

Another long-serving landlord was James Cowell, who kept the hotel from 1879 to 1893. James stated in the directories that he not only ran the Bay Horse, but was also the proprietor of a cab and coach service and the 'Working Men's Home'. James died in May the following year and was renowned for his help in times of distress and for providing soup kitchens for those in need. In the early nineteenth century, the Bay Horse was used for a brief period as a lock-up and during the Napoleonic War the hotel became a recruiting centre, when, it was stated, would-be recruits were tempted into service by five-pound notes. One of the last landlords was John W. Buck – older regulars might recall him. The name, of course, refers to any horse of a reddish-brown colour. In 1888, the Bay Horse was owned by Grimshaw's Brewery though it converted to a Massey's house when they took over Grimshaw's in 1927.

Bee Hive Inn*, 20 Marlborough Street, closed 1969

One of two inns of this name, this one was located on Marlborough Street near the appropriately-named Bee Street. Both this Bee Hive and the one on Holmes Street were Massey houses. This beerhouse, as it was in its early days, dated from about 1881, when Thomas Holden was keeping it. Thomas was assisted by his wife, Susannah, a Pendleside lass.

Bee Hive*, 5 Holmes Street, closed in 1969

This Bee Hive was almost directly across from the old Pentridge Cinema or 'Circulation Club'. The inn was kept by J. Capstick in 1923 and Christina Clough in 1945, when it is still listed under 'beerhouses'. I can remember the inn, which was pulled down during the construction of the flats complex known as Lower Tentre. The name Tentre, by the way, is a misspelling of 'Tenter', for long ago there were tenter fields here where cloth was stretched out on racks to dry. The name lives on with the saying, 'being on tenterhooks' when under strain or stress, as the cloth would be when drying.

Bee's Wing, Rodney Street

This inn was located in Rodney Street, which, along with Fountain Street and Fountain Court, was a tenement dwelling occupying the site of the Old Market Hall that was opened in 1870, and so the Bee's Wing predates that. A reference to the pub is made in the *Advertiser*, 24 December 1858:

> John Accornley, of the Bee's Wing beerhouse, Rodney Street, was summoned for having two men drinking in the house at a quarter past eleven on Sunday afternoon the 12th. The constable said that there were many complaints against this house for selling at unlawful hours. Fined 20s and costs.

The pub is mentioned by the *Advertiser* in connection with another court case on 1 October 1866:

> Elizabeth Salisbury was summoned for breach of the Beer Act. PC Lord stated that the defendant kept the Bee's Wing beerhouse in Rodney Street. He visited the house at half past eight on the night of 17 September. Preparing to go in, he stopped in the lobby as there was a hole in the wall, and looking through he saw several men playing cards. He saw them play two games for 6d and a pint of ale. He went in and seized the cards. The defendant was in the room and said that the cards belonged to a young man. She had not had a card in the house for the last three months, but her customers said that if she would not allow them to play cards they would go elsewhere. Fined 10s and costs. The defendant had been up seven times before, the last time she was fined 40s and costs.

I can't offer any explanation for the strangeness of the name – the Bee's Wing!

Big Window, see New Red Lion

Bird in the Hand, Lowerhouse Gate, closed 1926

This beerhouse was owned by John Simpson in 1854, and unusually was a free house, that is, not tied to any particular brewery; he could, in fact, sell whichever beer he wanted. It was still a free house in 1888, with a rateable value of £85 and went under the ownership of 'The Exors of W. Simpson', presumably some relation to the John above? The beerhouse appears to have continued under this name till around 1887, when Charles Ridehalgh was running the place. It was reported in January 1884, that:

> On Wednesday, Mr Edmondson, inspector of nuisance, under the Public Health Act seized three pieces of pork weighing in all 150 pounds at the Bird i' th' Hand public house, Lowerhouse, and considered it to be unfit for human consumption, had it conveyed away to Burnley, and made an application to Dr Briggs, the medical officer at the police courts for its destruction. Dr Dean, the medical officer, having examined it, commended it as unfit for food, and an order for its destruction was granted.

After this date, the inn became known as the Lane Ends, although for decades afterwards it was always referred to by the regulars as 'the Bird'. The inn and the old cottages were demolished in 1924, when the more-imposing 'New Lane Ends' was built on an adjacent site. The inn, situated between a row of cottages, was quite near the present-day Lane Ends Pub, at Lowerhouse.

The Black Bull at Lane Head, when the landlord was John Edmondson. Notice the Marsden Hospital in the background. (Towneley Art Gallery and Museum)

Bird in Hand, George Street?

There is some confusion as to just where this beerhouse actually was. There is an unnamed beerhouse at No. 4 George Street in 1868, run by James Hull. George Street was off the old King Street near Newtown Mill. The beerhouse is mentioned in court cases in 1863 when Duke Wilkinson was running it, but the address given is simply 'Newtown'. This extract is taken from the *Burnley Advertiser*, 25 April 1863:

> Breach of the Beer Act. Duke Wilkinson, keeper of the Bird in Hand, Newtown, was summoned for committing a breach of the above Act. PC Lord stated that about fifteen minutes past one o'clock on the morning of the 8th inst., he was on duty in Newtown. Hearing a great noise coming from the beerhouse, he looked through the shutter and saw three men inside drinking. He knocked on the door and told them that he was a constable. They refused to open the door, and he waited about half an hour to get in, but they still refused him admittance. The defendant's wife appeared, and in defence said that they had been so often imposed upon by persons knocking at the door and calling out, 'police', that they did not think it was a constable on that occasion. The Bench said that the house bore a very bad character, and if it was brought before them again, they would inflict a much larger penalty. Fined 10s and costs.

The Bench did not have to wait very long, as reported in the *Burnley Advertiser*, 12 September 1863:

> Duke Wilkinson of the Bird in Hand, Newtown was summoned for a breach of the Act on the 30th inst. PC Lord said that he visited this house at nine o'clock in the morning and saw the wife of the defendant fill a gill of ale for a man at the door. The man paid for the ale. The defendant's wife,

who appeared for her husband, said that she filled the ale for an old man, seventy years of age. She did not take anything for it. She asked the officer if she might fill it. PC Lord said that he saw the man pay for the ale. She did ask about filling it, but he said nothing in reply. Fined 5s and costs.

Black Bull Inn, Marsden Road, Lane Head

This fine old inn still survives at Lane Head. It was owned by the Exors of Edward Livesey in the 1880s, though tied to Alexander Bell's Brewery at Barrowford. One of the earliest references to the establishment is in 1792, when William Roberts ran the 'Black Bull Inn'. In 1824, James Allen was landlord there. The inn is much older than this, however; look for the datestone over the doorway, inscribed with 'R.E. 1778'. Its name also tells that it was once a farm. In October 1872, at a time when Halstead Halstead was landlord at the Black Bull, the *Burnley Gazette* tells us that Mr Hartley applied for the license of the Old Bull Inn (sic) Burnley Lane to be transferred from Halstead Halstead to his widow, Mary Halstead. There was no objection and the license was transferred. One James Edmondson kept the inn, around 1879, and ran it until 1890, when Jane Edmondson, presumably his wife, continued there until around 1902. Later that year the licensee was John Edmondson and his wife, Martha Ann. It was during their time at the pub that a serious incident occurred, resulting in the death of a tailor, Elijah Banks. In late November 1902, customers at the inn were roughly made aware that two men, John Ridehalgh, a collier, and Elijah Banks, had become engrossed in a heated argument. Banks had been in the pub since the early hours of the morning, drinking rum most of the day. Ridehalgh came into the pub about six o'clock to order a pint of bitter. He went into the taproom of the inn, where Banks was.

The two were apparently 'good friends' but soon started arguing between themselves. The affair came to a head when Ridehalgh called Banks some foul names. Both men stood up for confrontation, and Ridehalgh ran Banks against the taproom fireplace. Here they both fell on the fender, with Banks on top, and Ridehalgh underneath. Two of the regulars pulled the men apart, and Banks, who was bleeding from a wound to the head, was helped out of the pub. The customers settled down, thinking it was all over, when both men burst through the front door, fighting again. The fight continued in the lobby of the pub until both men were separated. Ridehalgh had Banks by the throat and was hitting him with his other hand. Banks, now bleeding from a number of wounds, was taken home by one of the patrons attending a party at the pub. John Ridehalgh was later charged with 'causing grievous bodily harm', though Banks died on the following Sunday morning and the charge was then the more serious one of 'manslaughter'. The inquest that followed was taken at the Cleaver Street police station, where, after hearing all the evidence, the jury returned a verdict of 'accidental death'. I'm reminded of some lads from the Black Bull who were playing don and dominoes at a location on the other side of town. When the game was over, they ordered a taxi to take them back to the Black Bull. The taxi arrived and the lads were deep in conversation, no doubt about the outcome of the game. One of them looked up and noticed they were fast approaching the Hapton interchange on the M65 motorway. 'This is not the way to the Black Bull,' he shouted out. The driver then replied, 'you don't want to go to Blackpool?' The driver obviously didn't understand the broad Lancashire dialect.

Black Dog Inn, 4 Cannon Street, closed in 1902

Another of those low-class beerhouses that were situated down 'Wapping' where Woolworth's car park is today down Hall Street, though at the Bridge Street end. The house was described

View of Cannon Street, showing the old Black Dog
on the right and Water Street on the left.
(Towneley Art Gallery and Museum)

The 'old' Blue Bell down Wapping. The couple sitting
down are thought to have been John Heaton and his
wife Ann. (Towneley Hall Art Gallery and Museum)

as being 'substantial' when John Eltoft was living there in 1800. Later, it was taken by John Hargreaves & Son of the Old Brewery, probably for warehouse storage, before finally becoming the 'Black Dog'. The inn was kept by a William Hopkins in 1820. He was a veteran of the Battle of Waterloo (June 1815) who was stated to be in receipt of a pension of 6d a day. William lost his fingers on the plains of Waterloo; he could not handle the reigns of his horse and so had to be discharged from the army. His wife, Hannah, was a Derbyshire lass, hailing from Glossop. Old William died in that house and is buried in St Peter's churchyard where the headstone can be seen to this day. Hannah lived several years afterwards, but left the business and lived a retired life after William's death. The inns and taverns in Wapping at this time were notorious for badger-baiting and reports indicate that this cruel 'sport' went on at the Black Dog as well as cockfights.

The beerhouse was rated at £34 in 1888 when it was owned by T. Horsfall of Brierfield. It appears to have ended its days around 1902 when Richard Binns is recorded as being the landlord. Richard was fined in May 1902, for serving ale to a drunken customer. Another landlord in the history of the inn was John Myers, who was a great sportsman in his day, and was considered one of the best hands at getting a cock bird for the fight in the country. It was said he kept the house well and never had a conviction against him during his long tenancy. They were a rough lot down Wapping, but John had his way of dealing with the 'rowdies'. He had a walking stick, a kind of bludgeon with which he argued matters with the rough customers. The name 'Black Dog' might have had some connection with badger-baiting, which was common at one time.

The pub is mentioned in the *Burnley Gazette*, 25 May 1872, in connection with, 'Alleged Felonies. A woman named Ellen Duffy, alias Birns, a tramp, was charged with stealing at the house of Job Myers, beer-seller in Cannon Street, last Saturday, a sum of money from the person of Peter Foxhall, a plate-layer'. The same newspaper reported again on Ellen Duffy as being a woman 'of low character, who was fined 20s and costs or, in default, one month's imprisonment' for assaulting PC Briggs. It appeared that the prisoner was apprehended on a charge of robbing a man (see above) and whilst being brought to the station she violently kicked the officer on the legs. The prisoner, of course, had no money, and she was marched off to prison.

One year later, the *Burnley Gazette* announced the sale of the pub on 3 May 1873:

> To be sold by auction by Mr A.G. Denbigh, on an early date, the whole of that well-accustomed beerhouse called the 'Black Dog', with the butcher's shop, warehouse, and other property situated at the corner of Bridge Street and Cannon Street, in Burnley. Further particulars may be had at the offices of the auctioneers, or Messrs Southern and Nowell, solicitors, Burnley.

Black Rock Inn, Trafalgar Road

I only have sparse information on this beerhouse and that is from a couple of court cases in 1859 and 1868. The beerhouse was on Trafalgar Road, the old name for Trafalgar Street at Thorneybank (that area near the Manchester Road railway station). On 29 June 1859, the Burnley Advertiser reported that, 'John Hargreaves of the Black Rock beerhouse was charged with supplying ale on Sunday morning the 16th inst. Fined 40s and costs'. The beerhouse was put up for rental in January 1868, as advertised in the *Burnley Advertiser*, 25 January 1868: 'beerhouse to let. To be let by tender, that well-accustomed beerhouse known as 'the Black Rock' situated in Thorneybank, Burnley. Tenders to be sent to Mr George Hargreaves, Padiham on or before Wednesday next, the 29th inst'.

Black Swan*, 3 and 5 Royle Road, closed 1924

A beerhouse, formerly known as 'Old Parr's Tavern'. R. Heap was probably the last landlord at the Black Swan, and the premises were on the viaduct-side of Bankhouse Street and on the corner of Royle Road. In the 1880s, J. Hargreaves and Son of the 'Old Brewery' (which was situated at the junction of Moseley Street and Bridge Street), owned the Black Swan. John and Jane Bowes were here at this time with their children, Sarah, Richard, Mary, Ellen and Clara.

Blue Bell, Wapping

The 'old' Blue Bell was at the far end of Wapping, at the bottom of Hall Street. In 1895, this building was a common lodging house, though previously it had been a pub, or beerhouse, and prior to that, a dwelling house. The building was demolished around 1914, although some of the structure on the right remained until about 1962. This inn was kept by John Heaton and his wife, Ann. Some time later, the same couple took another house in Wapping, and having obtained a license, called it the 'New Blue Bell'. The tenant after the Heatons was a Mr Brooks, who, after a few years here, left and went to Liverpool. Next came Thomas Greenwood, better-known by the name of Tom Steen, he was at the Blue Bell for many years. When he finally left, he bought a house on the corner of Boot Street and Croft Street, got a beer license and named it the Oddfellow's Arms. Later the Blue Bell had a cottage added to it, and then became known as the 'Farrier', or sometimes, the 'Horse and Farrier'. See that entry.

Boar's Head, 13 Temple Street, closed 1883

Apparently this was a short-lived beerhouse that was in existence between 1879 and 1883, run by William Carter and Greenwood Starkie respectively. Greenwood Starkie used to work as farm-hand at the Wholaw Farm near the top end of Manchester Road before taking on the Boar's Head beerhouse. By 1887, it had become the Tackler's Arms. See that entry also.

Boilermaker's Arms, Grimshaw Street

The Grimshaw Street reference is given in an old directory. I have little further information on this beerhouse, other than that, below, the building probably dates back to the middle of the nineteenth century. It is recorded in the *Burnley Advertiser*, 16 November 1861, that, 'Sam Dean of the Boilermaker's Arms beerhouse charged Sarah Thompson of the wilful damage of a square in one of his windows. Ordered to pay the damage and 6d costs'.

Boot Inn, 18 St James's Street, still open as Yates's Wine Lodge

The Boot Inn, or rather, Yates's, as we know the pub today, was built in 1911, although it is much older than this. Prior to 1800, it was originally the Boot and Shoe Inn, with a brewhouse for making their own ale, and was being tenanted by the Dents and rated at £7. Robert Dent was the 'victualler' in 1792, and a John Dent was living there with Martha (his wife?) in 1828.

The old Boot Inn, before rebuilding in 1911, was a much smaller building. (Briercliffe Society)

The Boot Inn today is known as Yates's Wine Lodge.

The Boot was put up for sale by auction on 28 August 1851 at the Swan Inn, and described as:

> Lot 1: All that messuage inn or public house called the Boot Inn with brewhouse, stable, gig house, smithy and large yard and frontage thereto belonging (being corner premises) adjoining Saint James' Street and Parker Lane, Burnley. Tenant: Anthony Simpson, Innkeeper.

This is one of the few of the older local inns that never had a farm attached. Alice Gray was running the Boot in 1861.

The pub features in an article from the *Burnley Advertiser*, 18 June 1863, which reports that, 'Ann Reed was charged with being drunk and riotous in St James's Street on Sunday night and breaking windows at the Boot Inn Vault. Fined 5s and costs, in default fourteen days' imprisonment. She stated that she was a widow and came from Carlisle'. Mrs Margaret Walton was the landlady at the Boot Inn in the mid-1890s; a decade previously she had worked as a housekeeper at the inn for her widowed sister, Betty Harrison, who was the landlady at that time. The inn was listed under Thwaites' houses in the late 1880s.

Borough Hotel, 14 Halstead Street

This public house on Halstead Street, beside the Manchester Road railway station, was obviously built to cater for the rail traveller. The hotel probably dates from around the late or early 1860s, and the name commemorates the Charter of Incorporation granted to the town in 1861. The landlord and landlady at the Borough in 1871 were William and Ann Howarth. The immediate area around the pub was called Thorneybank, a rather low-class district tenanted in the main by miners and weavers. The pub was long known as Burnley's only free house when most other inns and hotels were owned by the main brewery's, such as Massey's, Grimshaw's and Thwaites'. However, the inn was privately owned in the 1880s by J. Barker, although it was tied to Grimshaw's Ales, and listed under Massey's houses, probably from when Grimshaw's was amalgamated with the Massey Brewery in 1927. The *Burnley Gazette* of 9 January 1875 tells us that the license of the Borough Hotel was transferred to Richard Parker.

Bowling Green Inn, 25 Clifton Street, closed 1991

This former inn is still standing, but sadly no longer used for its original purpose, having closed in the early 1990s. When the militia barracks on Clifton Street were erected in 1854, for some time the men were drilled in a large room at the Bowling Green Inn, till the Wesleyan school at Keighley Green was secured. In 1958, what was thought to have been the first floodlit green in the North of England was opened by Fred Hartley, the licensee, watched by Jack Bolton, manager at Massey's Brewery. Illumination was provided by six 1,500-watt lamps fixed onto iron posts measuring 24ft high. Richard ('Dick') Layfield, a former Burnley footballer, was landlord here from 1893. He was succeeded by his son, also named 'Dick'. The Bowling Green was a Massey house in the 1880s, though it sold Burtonwood's ale just before its closure. Arguments rage as to whether or not the inn was ever the 'only pub in Stoneyholme'. It might have been for a brief period during Ward boundary changes. However, by a decree of the Tatton family, who owned the land, Stoneyholme was denied any public house.

The old Bowling Green
Hotel, just after its closure
in 1991.

Reports of one charitable landlord appeared in the *Burnley Advertiser*, 3 January 1863:

Mr Jesse Holdsworth of the Bowling Green Inn has, for the third time, given his Christmas treat
to the town's scavengers. On New Year's Eve, they sat down for a substantial supper to which
they did ample justice. They made a 'jolly good night of it' for which they gave their grateful
thanks to the host and the hostess.

Brickmaker's Arms*, 52 Yorkshire Street

According to a list of pubs and hotels published in 1888, this establishment was originally a
beerhouse known as the Bricklayer's Arms, owned by Massey's and rated at £35 5s. The name is
fitting, for that trade went on to the rear of the pub in the 1850s, although the first reference to the
pub is not until 1879. In fact, the land to the rear was known as 'Brick Field' and marked as such in
1851. Another 'Brick Field' was on the other side of the canal where the first Sainsbury's used to be.
The house is built from the product and material of the tradesman after whom it was named, and
bears the date 1898, when John Yates was the landlord here. The upgrading of the building would
allow the premises to have a publican license, thereby permitting the sale of spirits as well as ale.

Bridge Inn* Gannow Lane, still open as Gannow Wharfe

This pub is now aptly named the 'Gannow Wharfe', for directly to the rear is the canal, where,
on the opposite bank, the coal staith for the output of the local collieries in this area used to
be. There appears to be no evidence of the Bridge Inn being called the 'Pig and Whistle' or the
'Gannow Young Men's Mutual Improvement Society' as noted on a board outside the pub. The
Bridge Inn is mentioned in 1893 (although it is older than this) when James Hartley was keeping
it. It dates from at least 1858 (see the report of the court case below), although it might well
have been rebuilt since then. Although the inn has changed its name to the Gannow Wharf, the
words, 'Bridge Inn' still appear over the main door in stone.

The Bridge Inn on Gannow Lane is shown here during a weavers' strike at Woodbine Mill, probably in 1911. (Eric Hebdon)

Another reference to the inn can be found in the *Burnley Advertiser*, 22 May 1858:

James Taylor of the Bridge Inn, Gannow Lane was charged with a breach of the Beer Act. On Sunday 9th inst, the police constable found four men in the privy in connection with the house and, on going into the house, he found a man at the bar with a glass of ale. The defendant disclaimed all knowledge of the circumstances, saying that he had been upstairs and had just come down when the policeman entered. Fined 40s and costs.

Bridge Inn*, 2, Bank Parade, still open at the time of writing

The Bridge Inn of today stands on the site of a building originally known as 'the Dairy' and was rebuilt in 1905, (see datestone) by Guy David Louis Fernandes, whose initials can be seen inscribed in stone on the building. He married Mary Hargreaves, the daughter and heiress of John Hargreaves of the Old Brewery. Mr Fernandes died in 1916. The building replaced an older Bridge Inn, which, in 1888, was owned by the Exors of Samuel Howard, though it had to sell Old Brewery ale. The house in later years became one of the many Massey houses in town. By the mid-1890s, the Bridge Inn landlord was John W. Hoyle. In the 1920s, it was the house of Alf Bassnett, a popular Burnley FC half-back who later took over the license of the White Bull in Gannow Lane, where he remained until the 1950s.

Britannia Inn, 9 Roper Street – this inn's license lapsed in 1907

In 1868, this place is noted as being a beerhouse and was run at this time by James Baldwin. Roper Street was off the old Bridge Street near the Keighley Green. I am not sure whether the following court case, reported in the *Burnley Advertiser* (4 January 1868), refers to the Britannia on Roper Street or Oxford Road:

The old Bridge Inn on Bank Parade, when the landlord was Richard Benson. (Towneley Art Gallery and Museum)

A Dry Subject. Thomas Scarr, who keeps the Britannia beerhouse, Burnley was summoned for a breach of the Beer Act on Sunday morning 22nd December. PC Bracken said that at eight o'clock on the above morning he found a man in the defendant's house with a glass of beer before him. He was a native of Burnley. Defendant said that the man came to him and said that he was 'dry' and he thought a glass would do him no harm. He had not kept a beerhouse long and he was quite unaware of the custom. Fined 5s and costs, or in default, seven days.

Britannia Inn, 107 Oxford Road

This pub is named after the female warrior carrying a trident and wearing a helmet and personifying Great Britain. It dates from around 1890 when J. Moffatt was landlord there. The inn is a typical Lancashire pub and still survives after threats of closure some years ago, following demolition of a number of houses in the vicinity.

Bull and Butcher, Manchester Road

The Bull and Butcher is a classical roadside inn that still retains its coaching-look. Trade was greatly increased at the inn by the building of the present Manchester Road in the 1790s and, up to a short time ago, the Bull and Butcher still had a horse trough outside as a reminder of the horse traffic that once plied this old highway. Interestingly, the Habergham Eves Parish Council still hold their meeting at the Bull and Butcher. The inn was doubtless, in its early years, a farmhouse and the old trade of making clay pipes took place in a cottage next door to the pub. A name-change in December 2000 to the 'Slaughtered Lamb' brought many objections – happily it was changed back to the Bull and Butcher. It is now simply, the Bull. Padiham magistrates gave permission for the inn to be rebuilt in 1913.

The Britannia almost faced closure a few years back, but still survives as a typical local pub.

The old Bull and Butcher, before being rebuilt in 1913, seen in a more rural age. (Towneley Art Gallery and Museum)

Bull Hotel, 1 Manchester Road, closed 1932

Properly the 'Black Bull', which was situated at the foot of the present-day Manchester Road and directly across from the Red Lion, this pub once stood on the site now taken by Burton's tailors. The original building dated back to 1698, and was known as Black Bull Farm. The land in the immediate area towards the present-day town hall was known as 'Bull Croft'. Here were carried out the 'sports' of cockfighting and bull-baiting, the latter of which is thought to have given the name to the farm. The original inn was a lowly building in the style of a farm, to which a brewhouse and stables were attached, and its antiquity can be judged by the fact that in 1760-61, the Burnley churchwarden's accounts stated that 'paid to Mrs Nutter, Bull Inn, for proclamation expenses, £1 11s 8d'. A later building was built by Colonel John Hargreaves, the colliery owner, in 1817. The Bull was still listed in 1888 under the name Sir John Thursby, who succeeded to the collieries owned by John Hargreaves. The building of 1817 took more than a year to complete, due to a depression in trade, and soon acquired the title of 'the Folly' by the locals. The Bull soon became the meeting place for the governing bodies of the town, no doubt influenced by Colonel John Hargreaves who was the largest rate-payer in the Blackburn Hundred. In 1823, following Joseph Lee, came Mr James Allen as tenant of the Bull, and his name is listed in a directory for 1824. He hailed from Huncoat and later owned and kept the Mason's Arms. A postal service was at this time well established at the Bull, and Mr Allen improved this considerably, and in 1824 opened in competition to the Manchester coach service. Following Mr Allen, around 1830 came the Wilsons and their daughter, Ann, who in later years was to be wooed by the Bull's most famous landlord, Richard Rothwell. Dick was an excellent coachman and was soon employed on the Manchester run. His exceptional horsemanship was even noted by the General James Yorke Scarlett, who insisted on having lessons from the young man. Following the demise of the coaches with the coming of the railway in 1848, coupled with the death of Mr Wilson, Dick became licensee of the Bull Hotel. Dick was well liked and respected as mine host of the inn, and his untimely death on 23 January 1864 shocked the town, even though he had been ill for a number of weeks. His demise came just a few days before his forty-eighth birthday, and he was laid to rest at the parish church in a family vault. Cath Rothwell ran the inn for a time, until the Exors of John Hargreaves handed over the tenancy to Hannah Wallace. In 1871, the familiar structure of the 'new' Bull, with its door facing 'old gawmless' gas lamp, was constructed.

The *Burnley Express* reports on 6 August 1881 that, 'John McPollard was remanded for a period of eight days for stealing an overcoat from the saddle room of the Bull Hotel, belonging to Joseph Dean Whittam'. The Bull is mentioned a second time in with news that 'John McHale, French polisher, was fined 5 shillings and costs for being drunk and disorderly in the Bull Hotel Vaults on Monday. The constable who took the prisoner into custody was informed that he had assaulted several persons, but the prisoner called two witnesses to show that other parties were the aggressors'.

Bull's Head*, 25 Riding Street, closed 1978

These premises were originally a beerhouse, possibly opened by John and Jane Hughes, who were listed as the landlord and landlady in 1871. It was still classed as a beerhouse ten years later when John and Sarah Hargreaves were running the place. This modest little mid-terraced pub was associated with a number of 'characters', like the one who lived next door to the inn, who wore a black patch over one of his eyes. One day he was confronted by someone who he owed some money to, and swore he was penniless. The man decided to search him just in case, but still found nothing. Inside the pub, he lifted his patch and pulled out a ten-bob note. 'He never thought of looking there,' he beamed.

The Bull was an ancient hostel and occupied a prominent position at the bottom of Manchester Road. (Briercliffe Society)

Butcher's Arms*, 39 Market Street

This old beerhouse was situated on Market Street – a continuation of the bottom of Standish Street – before rebuilding went ahead during the 1960s. A stone over the doorway gave the date 1817, and a painted board stated 'Butcher's Arms, Old Brewery Ales'. The beerhouse was owned by the Corporation, who leased it to the Old Brewery. Shortly after 1888, the Corporation let the license lapse and from then, the building was used by the Market Department for storage. The building was demolished in April 1935. The last licensee was J. McConnell, a former Burnley footballer.

Caldervale Inn*, 6 Caldervale Road, closed 1939

This beerhouse closed in 1939 and the site it occupied is now taken by Focus DIY store, near the junction to Westgate. F. Shuttleworth ran the place in 1923, though its last landlady was Francis Ellen. Its close proximity to Massey's Brewery resulted in the firm opening their wine store next to the inn. When Caldervale Inn closed, a total of £1,900 was paid out in compensation. The building was formerly known as the 'Bridge End House' with a large garden, barns and a good stretch of land almost reaching the railway arches. Jonathan Peel, a relative of the more-famed Sir Robert Peel, lived here for a time. Robert Holgate, who entered into partnership with Lord Massey, thus founding the famous Massey Brewery, bought the property in later years.

Cambridge Inn*, 68/70 Oxford Road, closed in 1957

Quite a boozy little road is Oxford Road, which, besides its numerous pubs, had more than a few beerhouses. Alfred Duckworth was the landlord at the Cambridge Inn by the mid-1890s, although by the mid-1920s, Christopher Calvert was the mine host.

Canal Tavern, 63 Manchester Road, closed in 1973

The tavern keeper at the Canal in 1824 was John Holgate, but the pub dates from around 1800. It was one of the last inns in town to brew its own ale. The tavern was put up for sale by auction at the Bull Hotel at the bottom of Manchester Road on 26 October 1891 and advertised as:

All that free fully licensed public house known as the Canal Tavern, situated in Manchester Road and Finsley Gate, both in Burnley, now in the occupation of the Executors of the late Mr Tom Bradshaw. The house contains on the ground floor: bar, vault, commercial room, smoke room, general room, kitchen and scullery with excellent cellaring underneath. On the first floor there are four bedrooms, a sitting room and bathroom. Also all that brewhouse adjoining consisting of a store room, fermenting room, boiler house and mash room and chimney.

The Canal Tavern might have been purchased by John Schofield who was listed as being the landlord here in 1896. A peculiarity at the Canal Tavern was that you had to go down some steps to get into the vault of the inn, owing to the steepness of Manchester Road. The inn was probably built to cater for the bargees on the nearby Leeds and Liverpool Canal, hence its name.

The Caldervale Inn was, at one time, the home of Jonathan Peel, a relative of Sir Robert Peel. The Peel family also ran the print works which later became Burnley Paper Works. (Briercliffe Society)

Cattle Market, 10 Elizabeth Street

This sturdily-built pub is happily still standing and its name recalls the cattle and fairs that used to be held just across the way before the building of the police station in 1952-53. The inn dates from the mid-1860s, when Robert and Mary Harling were running it. It was here in 1868 that a quartet of misfits made their last call before returning home to Whip Street just up the road on Finsley Gate, where a quarrel began which resulted in a fatal stabbing.

Cheshire Cheese*, 8 Edward Street, closed 1907

This property was put up for sale and advertised in the *Burnley Gazette*, 25 April 1874:

> For sale, the beerhouse known as the Cheshire Cheese situated in Edward Street, Mill Lane, now in the occupancy of James Gregson as tenant thereof. Also, that cottage adjoining now occupied by Luke Suthers.

It is probable that William Briggs acquired the house from the auction sale, for he is listed as landlord here in 1879. Edward Street is off Bridge Street. The name is rather a strange one for a Lancashire pub!

Clifton Hotel*, 127 Padiham Road, closed 25 July 1971

The Clifton (a rather grandiose title to be bestowed on a modest little pub), stood on Padiham Road. The Clifton started off as a beerhouse around the early 1870s, when Sam and Elizabeth Dean were running the place. By the early 1880s, the Clifton Hotel was still a beerhouse being run by Charles and Ellen Greenwood, and in 1896 it was named the 'Clifton Hotel' and Crossley Pollard was the landlord. On the last night that the pub was open, Alan Collinge, the landlord, who had had his marriage reception there sixteen years previously, pulled the last pints, and all the regulars sang 'Auld Lang Syne'. A sad night indeed, but memories remain. This article in the *Burnley Gazette*, 30 March 1872, accounts for the pub's failure to obtain a music license:

> John Whittam, of the Clifton Hotel applied for a music license. Mr Alexander, in reply to the Bench, said he had no objection to the applicant, but he objected generally to any beerhouse having a music license, because he did not think they were calculated to promote good order in those beerhouses. The Bench, having considered the application, said that they thought the number of houses at present licensed were amply sufficient for the town of Burnley, and they refused all the applicants.

Clock Face Inn, 32 St James's Street, closed in 1960

This inn was adjoining the Bay Horse on St James's Street and the later building was distinguished by the bust of Bacchus, or Dionysus, perhaps appropriately enough the Greek god of wine, who, it is said, 'loosens care and inspires music and poetry'. Over the top of two of the bedroom windows were also Latin quotes, interpreted as 'drink wisely' and 'in wine is truth'. This was an ancient

Right: The Cattle Market, in more recent years, became famed for drinking after time before the licensing laws were changed, even though the police station was just across the way. One theory for this was that the police knew just where to go if ever they wanted to arrest certain persons.

Below: This is the old Clock Face Inn on St James' Street. The landlord at this time was James Cowling, which would date this photo to around 1908, just before it was rebuilt. (Briercliffe Society)

hostelry, although it was rebuilt in 1909-1910. In 1792, the innkeeper here was Thomas Brookes. In the later years, William Slater, father of George Slater, who built Clock Tower Mill, was serving the ale at the Clock Face. The older building was depicted as a lowly whitewashed structure – it was this building which was advertised for sale on 10 August 1803 in the *Blackburn Mail*:

> To be sold by auction, the Clock Face Inn, Burnley in the County of Lancashire on Monday evening, 25 August 1803, subject to such conditions as will be then produced. All that leasehold capital messuage and well accustomed inn with outbuildings thereto belonging situated in Burnley called and known by the name of the Clock Face Inn. Nine hundred years of the lease of which are yet to come unexpired under and subject to the payment of 4d per year during the term.

The landlord of the tavern in 1856 was George Davye, who, in addition to his inn-keeping, advertised a horse and hearse for hire, at terms to the newly opened municipal cemetery of 5s. The Clock Face Hotel, which faced demolition in 1963 to make way for the offices of the Pearl Assurance Co., had the clock over the entrance, despite the fact that the timepiece never registered the time in its later years. Like many licensed houses, the Clock Face was rebuilt more than once and, during the course of improvement in February, 1910, workmen uncovered the remains of an original old clock over the door lintel. The timepiece was reinserted in its original place along with the improvements, despite its lack of working parts. The last landlord of the old inn before it was rebuilt in 1910 was James Cowling. One landlord, John Catlow, will best be remembered for his work with Burnley FC where he served nearly twelve years as a director of the club. He took part in securing many top players of the day for the club, such as Teddy Hodgson from Chorley, and Bert Freeman. John Catlow died in November 1921 and was followed by Fred Gebhard. The *Burnley Gazette*, 25 May 1872, reports how:

> Michael Thornton was summoned for refusing to quit the Clock Face public house when requested to do so by PC Dillon at the instance of the landlady. Defendant said he had got too much whiskey. His head would not carry so much whiskey as it used to do. He was fined 2s 6d and costs, or seven days.

The pub features in an advert in the same publication, dated 17 April 1875:

> To be sold by auction, by Mr A.G. Denbigh, at the Bull Hotel, Burnley on Monday, the 3rd day of May 1875, at four o'clock on the afternoon, subject to such conditions of sale as shall then and there be produced, all that well accustomed public house called or known by the name of the 'Clock Face Inn' St James's Street in the Borough of Burnley, and late in the occupation of Mrs Davye, but now occupied by Mrs Deacon, with stables, brewhouse yard, outbuildings and appurtenances thereto belonging. The property is freehold and will be sold subject to the payment of an annual chief rent of £50. Further information may be had and a plan of the property can be seen on application to Mr W.H. Colbran, Colliery Offices, Burnley, or to Messrs Artindale and Artindale, solicitors, Burnley.

The *Burnley Express* contains another reference to the Clock Face on 21 January 1882:

> Zachariah Taylor was charged with being drunk and refusing to quit the Clock Face, St James's Street, on the previous night. Prisoner said he'd come from Staleybridge and had only

just arrived in Burnley. Mr Nowell (magistrate's clerk): 'you might have got drunk outside' (laughter). The prisoner was fined 5 shillings and costs.

Clock Tavern, Curzon Street

I am afraid that I knew absolutely nothing about this beerhouse and had no idea that it even existed until I came across the following newspaper article from the *Burnley Advertiser*, dated 25 February 1867:

> Breaking windows. John Greenwood summoned Harriet Greenwood, his daughter-in-law for breaking two panes of glass at his house, the Clock Tavern beerhouse, Curzon Street on the 12th inst. The defendant did not appear. PC Lord deposed to serving the summons in Colne, upon which she said, 'tell him [complainant] to go to h—l, he will never see me again'. Complainant said that on the above day, his daughter-in-law came to his house and commenced quarrelling with another woman. He put the former out of the house, whereupon she smashed two squares in the front window. The damage was 3 shillings. This was not the first time she had conducted herself thus; she had several times broken windows in his son's house. Fined 5s and costs, and to pay damage.

Clough Springs Hotel*, 8 Parker Street

Formerly the Traveller's Home, this inn surrendered its license in 1906. This beerhouse was owned by Alexander Bell, of the Clough Springs Brewery at Barrowford, hence the name. The 'hotel' is mentioned in a court case in the *Burnley Gazette*, 25 December 1875:

> Henry Baxter was charged under warrant with having assaulted Jno. Senior, landlord of the Clough Springs Inn, Parker Lane. The complainant said that on the 27 November, the prisoner and another went into his house worse for liquor. Complainant refused to fill them any drink, and told them to leave the house. He refused to do so, and got some drink from the customers who had it in their glasses. Complainant again asked them to go, and went towards the door when the prisoner pulled his (the complainant's) whiskers and drew out a quantity of hair. The defendant made no defence, and was fined 20s and costs, in default one month's imprisonment.

Coach and Horses*, 48b Church Street

The Coach and Horses is a mock-timbered building and was formerly named Adlington House, the home of Richard Chaffer. The landlord in the 1880s here was Samuel William Johnson, who was born in Derbyshire, and he was helped out by his wife Elizabeth. The Chaffers were responsible for much of the property in the Park district; they also owned Adlington Farm and worked the land up to the canal and Godly Lane (Ormerod Road) Bridge. The steep little lane at the right-hand side of the inn was formerly named Rakefoot, where at the bottom were some tanning pits, and a stepping stone over the river Brun to Keighley Green and beyond. Robert Douglas is the first landlord mentioned in directories and that is in 1872. Mr Uttley was the landlord here at the Coach and Horses around the early 1960s.

Coachmaker's Arms*, 2/4 Adelphi Street, closed in 1981

The house is listed, though not named at Nos 2 and 4 Adelphi Street in 1868, as a beerhouse run by Lawrence Whitham. Ten years later Joseph Bearshaw was the landlord here. The Coachmaker's Arms took its name from the firm of coach and motor builders, John Knape and Son who, at one time, had a garage on nearby Cuerden Street.

Coal Clough Hotel*, 19 Coal Clough Lane

This unpretentious little pub caters for the locals in and around the Coal Clough Lane area. The inn sign depicts the winding gear of a colliery; a suitable sign, for coal was mined in the distant past in the vicinity of Scotts Park, and at the very top of Coal Clough Lane and beyond at Hapton Valley Colliery. Coal Clough Lane takes its name from this fact. The inn probably dates from around 1883, when Matthew Wilkinson was the landlord. Matthew ran the pub with his wife Isabella. A lodger here in 1881 was Thomas Tomlinson, who described himself as a 'stone quarry man' and probably worked at the Pickup Delph Quarry across the road. In the early 1960s, the landlord here was J.H. Ingham.

Collier's Arms, 210 Accrington Road

Closed around the mid-1880s, when it was renamed the Tradesman's Arms, see also the entry with this name. This beerhouse was kept by James Sagar from 1879 to 1883. James Sagar classified himself as a 'beer-seller and butcher' and lived at the house with his wife Elizabeth, their three sons and two daughters. Perhaps the beerhouse got its name from the fact that James Sagar took in lodgers who worked at the pit, such as his brother, John and boarder, George Farrah, who were both coal miners. The Collier's Arms was situated on the corner of Collier Street and Accrington Road. This used to be a small street, almost directly across from the Fleece Inn until it was demolished around 1912-14. In 1923, the beerhouse was occupied by E. Brownwood, an auctioneer, just after the license lapsed for what was then the Tradesman's Arms.

Commercial, 133 St James's Street, closed in 1962

The Commercial was another old inn on St James's Street, though its taproom entrance lay on Brown Street, the site of which is now taken by the Garden Bar. There appears to have been an inn of this name as far back as 1825. The Commercial is mentioned in a directory of 1848, when James Hartley was running the inn at Cheapside, this being the old name for this part of St James's Street. In the early 1860s, the Commercial was run by William Moor, 'victualler and blacksmith', along with his wife, Betty. There was a court case related to the Commercial taproom, reported in the *Burnley Advertiser*, 9 July 1864:

> Peter Hunt was summoned by his wife, Elizabeth Hunt for assaulting her on the Tuesday night previous. She keeps the Commercial Inn tap. She stated that, on that night named, he was in the tap and wanted to stay. She refused to let him, on which he kicked her, and she then got a poker and struck him on the back with it. She had got protection from the Bench some time

The Coal Clough pub still exists on Coal Clough Lane and, in recent years, has won awards for its beer.

before. The defendant said that he had not touched her, and that since she had got protection, she had approached him for money which he had given her. This she denied. The magistrates told her that the protection was no use to her so long as she did not keep a house of her own, and advised her to leave the tap, where she had only been a short time, and go into a house of her own. Her children (three boys) were in the centre of temptation where she was, and for their sake she ought to give up the tap. Fined 1s and costs, in default to be imprisoned for seven days.

The Commercial Hotel closed its doors on Thursday, 13 December 1962. Joe Whittaker, landlord for the previous half-century, pulled the last pints at a crowded house. There was a strange incident at the Commercial in July 1874, when the body of a newborn child was found in a septic tank at the rear of the pub. After some disagreement amongst the jury, a verdict was returned of 'wilful murder'. In the 1880s, the Commercial was owned by the Exors of R. Roberts, and served beer from the Old Brewery, though in later years it was a Massey house. The Exors of R. Roberts owned a number of 'pubs' in the town, including the Millstone.

Commercial Hotel, 8 Grimshaw Street, closed in April 1925

This building is still standing, though not used for its original purpose on Grimshaw Street. Known locally as Cronkshaw's, it was, for decades, used by the local liberals being especially renowned for its New Year's dinners. The property belonged to the daughter of Mr and Mrs Dugdale of Rosehill House – in fact, the small street next to it is called Dugdale Street. Although the building has now been taken as offices, it still retains the look of an old Burnley hotel.

Corporation Arms*, 47 Curzon Street, closed in 1967

The Corporation Arms was at the gable end of Garden Street and facing the bridge over the Brun. Originally a beerhouse, the Corporation was listed but not named at No. 47 Curzon Street in the 1861 census. At this time, the landlord was Ben Stevenson. Today this site is marked by the amusement arcade. This popular free house was actually tied to both Massey and Grimshaw. The premises were owned by Burnley Corporation and had been earmarked for demolition for over seventy years at the time of its closure in April 1967. During the whole of that time, the tenancy had had to be applied for and granted every three months, and one wonders if the name of the house was the outcome of this arrangement. Its age was a mystery, but the property was thought to date back to at least the early nineteenth century, and there was evidence that, at one time, it had been a series of cellar dwellings, for three fireplaces with ovens were fixed in the cellar. The inn had been in the hands of the Wilkinson family for over a century – grandfather, son and grandson, all named James, holding the license in turn.

Corporation Hotel, 31 Oxford Road

Thomas Bancroft was landlord of the Corporation on Oxford Road in 1872 and the inn probably dates from a little earlier than that era and the incorporation of the town in 1862. By the early 1880s, the Corporation was being run by John and Mary Barnes, who lived at the pub with their four sons and three daughters. This hotel still survives on Oxford Road.

Cottage in the Wood*, 5 Springfield Road, closed in 1973

The 'Cottage', as it was known locally, was a popular little pub along with its sister pub, the Owl in the Wood – the 'wood', of course being Burnley Wood when it really was a wood. The Cottage in the Wood dates from around 1879, when Henry Chambers was running the inn.

Craven Heifer*, (Falcon) 17 Holden Street

The house was originally an unnamed beerhouse of the 1860s, run by Peter Hargreaves. Peter Hargreaves was charged under breaches of the Beer Act in 1863. His trial was recorded in the Burnley Advertiser, 18 June 1863: 'Breach of the Beer Act. Peter Hargreaves was charged with serving beer to persons in his house at five minutes past one o'clock on Monday morning. Fined 10s and costs'.

The Corporation Arms served a good variety of ales, as can be seen from this picture. (Towneley Art Gallery and Museum)

The Corporation on Oxford Road probably dates from around the time of the incorporation of the town in 1862.

The inn is fittingly named after a cow, for this area was long-known as the 'Meadows' and still is by many locals residents. Also close by is Cow Lane, as a reminder of when it really was meadowland. The original address of the pub was No. 17 Holden Street (a reminder of the time when the front door was in this street) though today it is No. 1 Whittam Street. The inn is not named as such in the early 1880s, but it was the home of beer-sellers Thomas and Martha Nutter. The landlord here in 1945 was Thomas Martin, who later went on to the Yorkshire Hotel. The pub today has forsaken its original name and is now called the 'Falcon'.

Cricketer's Arms*, 51/53 Anne Street, closed in 1972

Originally a beerhouse, named the 'Live and Let Live' in the early 1860s, the building was later a grocer's shop and beerhouse run by William Stowell. Later it became the Joiner's Arms run by William Greenhalgh, though unnamed in 1868, and by Ethelbert Pate in 1879. Ethelbert was ably helped around the beerhouse by his wife, Rose Hannah. It became the Cricketer's Arms in about 1883, though still run by Ethelbert Pate. The name was much more fitting in view of the close proximity to Burnley Cricket Ground.

Cricketer's Arms*, Lowerhouse Gate, closed in 1985

The pub landlord here in 1879 was Edward Capstick and the pub was owned by the Exors of Henry Whittaker in 1888, and sold Massey ales. Edward Capstick, his wife Lucy and their three daughters were still at the beerhouse a couple of years later. This cosy little inn was situated at No. 108 Lowerhouse Lane. One of its landlords was the popular Lowerhouse cricketer (appropriately enough), Tommy Shutt. Another cricketer-landlord was Sam Howarth from 1922 to 1924. Such was his zest for fitness that, his over-training resulted in a heart condition, from which Sam was to die at the early age of thirty-seven years.

Cross Gates*, 2/4 Coke Street, closed in 1915

The license for this beerhouse lapsed in 1915 and a total of £2,100 was paid in compensation. The premises however, weren't demolished until 1953, when a board over the doorway was discovered proclaiming that, 'Thomas Walmsley was licensed retailer'. It was Gibson's fish shop in the 1920s. Coke Street was off Finsley Gate just beyond Parker Lane coming from the Manchester Road end of Finsley Gate. The beerhouse, in 1888, was owned by Maria Tattersall, and was a free house not tied to any particular brewery. Maria appears to have had the place almost since its inception around 1878. Thomas Walmsley ran the place from 1896 to around 1902, but, in spite of the old inn sign, the last landlord was probably John Chapman.

Cross Guns*, 52 Gannow lane, closed in 1955

This little inn was located just beyond the junction with Cog Lane, going down Gannow Lane towards the Grey Mare. The beerhouse in the mid-1880s was being run by Thomas Campbell. The last landlord here was probably Ben Constable. The *Burnley Gazette*, 10 July 1875, reports:

The old Cross Gates Inn on Coke Street. The sign on the low building reads: 'Thomas Walmsley. Licensed to sell ale and porter to be consumed on the premises. Tobacco'. (Briercliffe Society)

John Harris, landlord of the Cross Guns beerhouse, Gannow Lane, was summoned for having his house open at 11.15 p.m. on the 25th inst, and James Hudson and others for aiding and abetting. The case was fully proved and the Bench fined Harris 20s and costs and the others 2s 6d and costs.

Cross Keys Inn, 150 St James's Street

In 1824, James Rawcliffe was the tenant listed at the Cross Keys, and three years later, someone I presume to have been his widow put the inn up for sale. At the time, the inn was described as:

All that old established and well accustomed inn or public house, the sign of the cross keys with a brewhouse, three stables with hay lofts, one large barn with shippons and other suitable outbuildings in the occupation of Mrs Rawcliffe, together with two cottages adjoining. The last lot in the occupation of Mr Alston, tailor, and Mr Moorhouse.

Although rebuilt in 1906, the hotel is reputed to hark back to 1750. In its early days, the pub was known as the White Horse – a name surrendered in 1791. The town's only church at that time was St Peter's. Perhaps the change to Cross Keys had some significance, the cross keys being the symbol of St Peter?

In 1865, the hotel became a sub-post office, a facility that lasted about ten years. During the days when the Margerison's were working the Burnley Print Works, large numbers of their men employees claimed a room at the inn as their own and received their wages here. Here, the 'block printers' were said to be on good money and it's fair to say that most of it went on ale. The inn, around the late 1880s, was privately owned by the Exors of James Topper, though it served Massey ales. The Cross Keys in 1953 boasted that it was appointed by the RAC and that all the bedrooms were fitted with hot and cold running water, and central heating. Harry Nuttall was landlord at this time.

The old Cross Keys Hotel, before being rebuilt in 1906: notice the old public toilet on the bridge over the river Calder. (Briercliffe Society)

Crown and Kettle, Howe Street, and the Old Market Hall site

This beerhouse was apparently near to the Old Market Hall, and originally it was a fish shop kept by 'Old Carter'. Some time afterwards it was changed into a grocer's shop and kept by Hargreaves Hargreaves. A third storey was leased to Mr Georgeson for use as a cabinet-maker's shop. One night it all burnt out, and ruined Hargreaves. Afterwards, it was repaired and opened up as the beerhouse by John Driver, a tinner who lived next door with the tin shop in the cellar of the house he lived in. He moved to the Crown and Kettle, and a while after he bought the old sign of a redundant beerhouse in Roberts Row, named 'General Williams, the Hero of Kars' – the former name of the General Williams, Manchester Road. The sign was placed over the Crown and Kettle, and it became 'General Williams, the Hero of Kars'. The house again changed tenants and was renamed 'Uncle Tom's Cabin'. It remained under this title (and is mentioned under the new name in a court case) until it was swept away for the building of the Old Market Hall, which opened in 1871. A court case connected with the pub was covered by the *Burnley Advertiser*, 11 April 1863:

Assault. James Gorden, weaver, was charged with assaulting Harriet Greenwood, the wife of William Greenwood, keeper of the Uncle Tom's Cabin beerhouse, Howe Street on Tuesday the 31st inst. He went into the house in question, and called for a pint of ale. He began to knock the table with the pot, and when the complainant told him to behave he called her names and struck her. She pushed him away and ran into the kitchen; he followed her, threw her down, and tried to get his hand into her pocket. He was then seized and taken away from her. He afterwards raised a crowd around the door and used threatening language. She was afraid and ran out of the back door. He was drunk and excited, and when seen by the police bleeding very

In the early 1960s, T. Jackson was the manager, as can be seen from the advert. Look for the ornate carvings around the door of the present building and the date of rebuilding, oft missed.

much from the head. Two witnesses appeared on behalf of the complainant. The prisoner said, in answer to the charge, that the complainant had struck him several times with the tongs, and if it had not been for the interference of the police he would have been 'slaughtered I'th hoil'. When asked if he had brought any witnesses he made reply, 'oi thowt oi'd browt mi' witness when I browt mi' yed' [I thought I had brought my witness when I brought my head]. The Bench fined him 10s and costs, in default he was committed to prison for one month.

The *Burnley Gazette* mentions another incident on 25 December 1875:

Maria Pomfret was in custody for having been drunk and incapable in Howe Street on Saturday night. PC Northover proved the case and said that the prisoner was so helpless that he had to take her to the lock-up in a wheelbarrow. In consequence of the prisoner having been in the lock-up from Saturday night, and in consideration of the facts stated by the superintendent of the police, namely, that nothing had been known against her since 1871, and that she earned her living by honest industry, the Bench discharged her.

Crown Inn, 34 Bridge Street, closed in 1962

This beerhouse developed from an unnamed beerhouse of 1868, at No. 30 Mill Lane – the old name for higher Bridge Street. It was being run at this time by George Boland. James and Jane Booth were the landlord and landlady of the Crown in 1865 and both were mentioned in a court

45

case that year. Jane was still the landlady in 1875 when the license was transferred from her to Henry Nuttall. It was noted in the *Burnley Gazette*, 15 May 1875 that, 'the license of the Crown Inn was transferred from Jane Booth to Henry Nuttall'.

Derby Arms*, 29 Standish Street, closed in 1953

This modest little pub stood where the Carlton is now; in fact, the inn and an adjoining property were demolished and the Carlton built in its place. The Derby Arms was originally an unnamed beerhouse at this address in 1868, being run by Eli Chew, who by 1879 had gone to the Commercial. Another landlord was John Alexander Christie, DCM, a native of Belfast who joined the army at the age of sixteen. He served in the Boer War and in India, returning to Burnley as an instructor in the Territorial in 1910. On the outbreak of the First World War, he accompanied the East Lancashire Regiment to Egypt, where he served in Gallipoli. Later, he became attached to the 9th Manchester Regiment, being promoted to RSM in 1919. Wounded no less than four times, he was awarded the DSM in 1917, and other medals. After completing thirty-two years' service he came back to Burnley to take the license of the Derby Arms in 1919, a place which he occupied until the time of his death in September 1934.

Derby Hotel*, 44 Grimshaw Street, closed in 1958

In the early 1870s, the Derby Hotel was run by John and Mary Ann Blakey. In the early 1880s, it passed to Edward Nutter and his American wife, Mary. The inn was closed down in 1958, but was not demolished until 1963, to make way for the then new bus station. A popular landlord here for twelve years, from 1915 to 1927, was Oliver Shambrook. Oliver was considered to be one of the fastest sprinters in the district, and had run against some of the best in England.

Derby Hotel, 177 Padiham Road

Now this hotel stands in isolation, set back from the once-busy Padiham Road. The pub is located in the old part of Padiham Road that was cut through with the building of the motorway. The Derby at Gannow Top dates from the early 1870s, when Peter and Ellen Whittaker were running the place. Landlord at the Derby for seven years from 1900 to 1907 was Ben Whitaker, a Burnley lad, though brought up at Halifax. Ben was a watchmaker by trade and kept a shop on Westgate for a time before entering into the licensing trade at the Derby. He was a keen bowling man, and at one time was secretary of the Clifton Bowling Club.

Recorded in the *Burnley Gazette*, 30 March 1872 was the following 'case of insulting language':

Susan Whittaker summoned Ann Hall for using insulting and abusive language. Mr Nowell appeared for the complainant and Mr Hartley for the defendant. Complainant is the wife of Peter Whittaker, who keeps the Derby Hotel, Habergham Eves. The defendant was her husband's daughter. Defendant and three others of her husband's children went to her house last Thursday night, between seven and eight o'clock. She called her a bad name and threatened to pull her liver out. Stones were also thrown at the door for three quarters of an hour. By Mr Hartley – Defendant was outside the house. I saw the defendant at the front door. They came about a girl who left the house

The only known photo of the Derby Arms shows the Home Guard marching past, which is suitable as a former landlord, John A. Christie, had a long and proud army record. (Briercliffe Society)

and went to her sister's. Sarah Jane Taylor, a lodger at the house, said she saw the defendant at the door. She corroborated as to the bad language used. Mr Hartley asked the opinion of the Bench on the Act of Parliament under which the charge was brought. He said it was under police regulations, and he wished to know if the information should not have been laid, either by a policeman or a Corporation Officer? Peter Whittaker junior was then called. He said that Mrs Hall was taking his youngest sister home. The lodger called his sister foul names. By Mr Nowell – I have just been bound over to keep the peace towards my father. Three sisters went to the door, and I stood in the road watching. My sister called my father 'an old murderer'. I heard my sister call my stepmother a ------. In reference to the point raised by Mr Hartley, Mr Nowell said that the Act belonged, not to the Corporation, but to everybody in Burnley, and everybody could take advantage of it. He also said it was a very great advantage, as it saved much expense, in not having to serve writs for insults like this. The Bench said it was a great disgrace to all parties, and dismissed the summons.

Derby Inn*, 1 Tunstill Street, (old address, now on Colne Road)

Notice the carving over the door on the Tunstill Street side of the building, 'A. W.' – probably the initials of Angelo Waddington, architect. In April 1981, a long-serving landlady of twenty-five years at the Derby gave some interesting reminisces on her retirement. She recalled 'Scouce' the parrot, who used to order two pints at a time and had a vocabulary to equal that of any used in the taproom of the pub. Then there was the nine-inch alligator she bought for her husband that grew to nineteen inches before biting through the electric wiring heating its tank on the bar. 'It did a flip, a back somersault, and then died,' she said. The last pint she pulled was for Bill Acornley, who celebrated his seventy-eighth birthday on the same day she left the pub. A fitting tribute, for Bill was the first customer she served when she took over the pub. Following her retirement, the pub was taken over by Mr and Mrs Bob Miller, who moved there from the nearby Duke of York Hotel.

Devonshire Hotel*, 9 Boot Street, closed in 1958

The Devonshire Hotel, with the old Pickup Croft School standing next to it, was near the present-day bus station. In fact, the inn was demolished in 1963 to make way for the development in this area (then known as Pickup Croft). One of the earliest references to this beerhouse was in 1868, when, though unnamed, it was still at No. 9 Boot Street. The landlady at this time was Ellen Smith. Every town it seems has a 'Devonshire'; this one was probably named after the Duke of Devonshire. By the early 1880s, the widow Sarah Wilkinson was running the inn, which was at this time still unnamed. She was there with her three stepdaughters – Sarah, Mary, and Emma – and two stepsons, Alfred and Moses.

Dog and Duck, 95 St James's Street, closed in 1959 (or 1962?)

One reference to its closure is given as 1959, although the Dog and Duck is mentioned in a directory for 1962 – the landlord then being R.H. Cunliffe. The place, it seems, always had an unsavoury reputation, to be avoided by the more decent members of society. The inn, given a name that recalls the hunting days, was quite old, being listed in a directory of 1848. At this time, George Watson was running the place, though its address then was 101 St James's Street.

The Derby Hotel, in a quieter age, can be seen on the right of this photo and is on the corner of Padiham Road and Boat Horse Lane. Here the barge horses were taken over from the Cog Lane end of Gannow Tunnel on the Leeds and Liverpool Canal to the Whittlefield end of the tunnel.

By the early 1860s, George and Ann Roper were running the Dog and Duck. Tales are told of a local character who I will name Nellie B---- who used to frequent the Dog and Duck, and who one night was listening intently to the gossip going on between the menfolk. 'I can pee higher up the wall than any man in this pub,' boasted one fellow – a typical pub argument of the day. 'Nay, you can't,' said another. 'Let's go and see then, and we'll have a bet on it,' said the first man. With that, Nellie jumped up and said, 'I can pee up the wall higher than any of you fellows – outside now!' The men lined up against the wall for this very important bet and got themselves ready for the challenge. Nellie then cocked up her leg, and at the last moment, said to the menfolk, 'remember now, holding'. She, of course, won the day.

The Dog and Duck is mentioned in the *Burnley Gazette*, 16 November 1872:

Bridget Mallay summoned Margaret Walsh for assault. Complainant said the defendant hit her three times on the face with her fist in the Dog and Duck public house. The reason for the assault was that the defendant's husband asked complainant to sup up, and the defendant said he would not do that, and she commenced to assault complainant. Complainant had not spoken to the defendant for three years. In reply to Mr Baldwin, she said she was not drunk. Thomas Ingham corroborated complainant. Mr Baldwin appeared for the defendant, and said he was instructed to say that the complainant's case was very much exaggerated. Bridget Lavin on behalf of the defendant struck complainant once, but it was only in consequence of complainant saying she could fight defendant. Fined 10s and costs, in default fourteen days. Defendant: 'Write my committal out, I'll go to prison'.

Dog and Partridge*, 90 Westgate, closed in 1964

This pub was in the private hands of Hubert Slater in 1888, but sold Massey's beers. The building dated from the 1870s. In 1879, William Chew was landlord of the beerhouse along with his wife, Elizabeth. The site of the Dog and Partridge today is the car park on the corner of Westgate and Arthur Street. One of the last landlords or landladies was H.A. Batchelor in 1962.

Dog and Rat, 48 Bankhouse Street

This was a beerhouse situated on Bankhouse Street from around 1861 through to the early 1870s and run by Ezra Dean (who also worked as a labourer in an iron foundry) and his wife, Elizabeth. It appears to have been on the site of the later Parkinson's Pill Factory, or maybe on the Royle Road side of the mill. The beerhouse is unnamed in the directories of 1868, though the address is Bankhouse Street. The name might be a reference to the rat pit the inn had, and if it existed today when everything must be grammatically correct, might have been named the 'Canine and Rodent'.

Dragoon, Hebrew Road: this pub appeared to have been closed for a time when I viewed it in 2007

'The Drag', as it is called locally, dates from around 1868 when James Haworth was running the inn. The inn name is a reference to General Scarlett and his Dragoon Guards. The landlord here in the early 1880s was Hugh Kirk and his wife, Eliza. The Coates family ran the pub for many years, namely James and Thomas.

Duke of York, 61 Colne Road

This ancient hostelry dates from at least the 1820s, though it has since been rebuilt, of course. Luke Scott is listed as landlord in 1824 and James Scott in 1828. The Duke of York we know today was constructed in 1881, although extended later and opened just before Christmas, in time for the forthcoming celebrations. The architect for the new building was Mr T. Bell. At the time, the pub was one belonging to Grimshaw's Brewery. Although 'Grimshaw's Sparkling Ales' can still be seen on a number of the pub windows, 'the Duke' was later acquired by Massey's. The pub is now centralised in the gyrator system, but at one time you could still drive on either side. When the Burnley Militia was formed in 1853, the men paraded and practiced in a field near the Duke of York Hotel three times a day. One of the landlords at the Duke from 1848 to 1854 was Law Brown, who married Mrs Keirby, the widow of a member of the brewing family. He came to an untimely end by hanging himself in the brewery's Church Street premises. The *Burnley Express* reports a similarly shocking incident in the history of the Duke on 18 June 1887:

> Shortly before ten o'clock on Wednesday morning, the neighbourhood of Duke Bar was startled by the collapse of an old building which formed the stable and scullery of the Duke of York Inn. It had been proposed to alter the premises, which are situated between the principal buildings and the old toll house which form a portion of the same block, and convert them into a vault for the inn with one frontage to Colne Road, and the other to Briercliffe Road. The work was under the supervision

of Mr T. Bell, architect, and was being carried out by Messrs Laycock and Sons, contractors. Mr Bell and Mr Laycock senior were, however, absent from town at the time of the occurrence of which we write. It was intended to place a cellar underneath the proposed vault. The floor of the old building had been removed, and excavations for the cellar were in progress and it is supposed that it was owing to inadvertence in getting the excavations too near the outer wall – that which fronts on to Briercliffe Road, it suddenly gave signs of being insecure. The workmen engaged in the work have frequently noticed rats on the premises, and on Wednesday morning, Mr Laycock junior, attracted by a noise which he attributed to one of these rodents, went to investigate. He then noticed a crack in the causeway, and saw unmistakable indications of the collapse of the building. He immediately called to the seven workmen who were in the cellar to leave the place, which they did by ascending a short ladder, leaving by an exit on the Colne Road side. They had only just succeeded in making good their escape, when the wall on the Briercliffe Road side was seen to bend in the centre, and to fall, carrying with it half the roof with a tremendous crash. The upper portion and the roof fell into the road, whilst the lower portion was deposited where the men had just left.

Empress Bar and Grill Chancery Walk, closed in 1984

This 'new' bar, surely one of the last to be built by Massey's, was opened in March 1961. The bar offered the customer anything from a quick snack to a full-blown meal. The varied bill of fare contained anything from a hamburger at 1s 6d, to spit-roast chicken, French fries and tomatoes. The chef at the time of the opening was Mr James McManus, who was formerly at the Keirby Hotel. The new bar was constructed on the site of the old Empress Hotel, and contained a lounge on the ground floor, with the dining room above on the second floor. The new manager at the bar room was Gerald Chadderton, former assistant manager at the Keirby. The premises, which still exist, though now taken over by retail shops, were built by Howarth Construction.

Empress Hotel, Chancery Street, closed in 1958

This grand, imposing building was another of those demolished to make way for the new market in 1958. The hotel appears to date from the 1890s, when Fritz Weber was running the place. The Empress Hotel 'Market Place, facing the Market Hall' in 1953 stated that, 'it was the most centrally-situated house in Burnley, had two lounges, writing rooms etc.'

Dick Lindley, a member of the Burnley cup-winning side of 1914 was landlord of the Empress in 1923. The building was designed by a young Burnley architect of the late nineteenth century, Charles Parsons, who died at the early age of thirty-seven.

Exchange Hotel, Nicholas Street, closed in 1948

These premises, which still exist, were actually at first the headquarters of the local branch of the Oddfellows, although the Exchange Hotel, dates from around 1870, when it was run by Samuel and Catherine Sefton. A decade later, the hotel was being run by manager, William Holyoak and his wife, Jane. The hotel was kept from 1914 to 1945 by the popular Tom Jackson. On surrender of the license in 1948, the building was taken over by Burnley Corporation and now accommodates various borough departments. The following notice appeared in the *Burnley Gazette*, 7 August 1875:

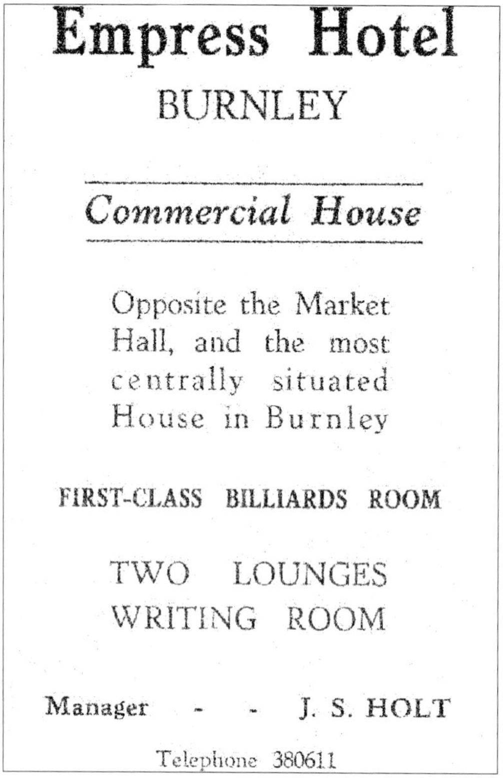

Empress Hotel

BURNLEY

Commercial House

Opposite the Market
Hall, and the most
centrally situated
House in Burnley

FIRST-CLASS BILLIARDS ROOM

TWO LOUNGES
WRITING ROOM

Manager - - J. S. HOLT

Telephone 380611

The Empress Hotel was, according to this advert, the most centrally-situated house in Burnley.

To Brewers and others. To be sold by tender or private treaty, all that large, commodious, and well accustomed public house, called the Exchange Hotel, now in the occupation of Peter Calvert, situated in Nicholas Street and Elizabeth Street, Burnley, in close proximity to the post office, Mechanic's Institution and Exchange, and other public buildings, together with the stables and coach house, and also the buildings intended as part of and adjoining the said hotel, being in the occupation of Francis Hartley, solicitor, and the Burnley Weavers' Association. Intended purchasers are invited to inspect this valuable property, and to send their tenders, under seal on or before the 31 August, to either the undersigned, from whom further particulars may be obtained. Mr John Fingland, Manufacturer, Whitefield New Mill, near Manchester: Mr George Gill, Lancashire and Yorkshire Bank Limited, Burnley, or W. T. Read, solicitor, 9 Hargreaves Street, Burnley.

Finsley Inn*, 58 Finsley Gate, closed 1928

This inn, or more properly, beerhouse, was located on the left-hand side of Finsley Gate, roughly where the bowling alley premises are today. The license for this beerhouse was surrendered in 1928, when a total of £2,250 was awarded in compensation. The inn was not named as such in the early 1880s, but the address was the same and it was then being run by Robert Brunton, with help from his son, also named Robert, who described himself as being an 'assistant beerhouse-keeper'. The beerhouse was a free house in the late 1880s when it was owned by the Exors of Thomas Lonsdale. The last landlord here was Mr William Sharples.

The Empress Hotel tap, when William Fegan was landlord there in 1914. (Towneley Art Gallery and Museum)

Fleece Hotel*, 213 Accrington Road

This hotel was originally a beerhouse dating from the late 1870s when it was being run by Francis Parker, who went on to run the place until 1896. Francis was still landlord in 1888, though the house was owned by J. Rawstron and selling William Astley (Nelson) beer.

Flying Dutchman*, Engine Street, closed in 1908

The license for this public house lapsed in 1908. The premises of the Flying Dutchman were located off Church Street, in the old Hill Top area and a sum of £1,100 was paid out in compensation when the beerhouse closed.

Footballer's Arms*, 55 Yorkshire Street, closed in 1968

Originally the Eastgate Inn ('Eastgate' being the old name for Yorkshire Street), this pub is mentioned as such in the following report, taken from the *Burnley Gazette*, 11 December 1875:

> Henry Harrison was summoned for an assault on Jane Simpson of the Eastgate Inn. Mr Sutcliffe appeared for the complainant and Mr Baldwin for the defendant. Complainant stated that on the 22nd Ult. Defendant went in and began to use abusive language, and she ordered

The Forester's Arms evolved from two terraced houses, as can be clearly seen from this photo – an 'Arms' being simply a meeting place.

him out, and he then knocked her head twice against the ceiling. Ellen Wilkes said defendant struck complainant over the head. A witness for the defence swore that complainant struck the defendant with a draught board, the case was dismissed.

A fire at the inn on 23 July 1968 spelt the end of the pub; the site is now taken by a bookmaker's.

Forester's Arms*, 49 Todmorden Road

The Forester's Arms, in close proximity to Burnley Wood, must have some connection with the foresters who worked there when it was Towneley land. John Chadwick was running the inn in 1868 and in 1879; although at the former time the beerhouse was unnamed but listed on Fulledge Road (the old name for Todmorden Road). John Chadwick ran the inn with his wife, Elizabeth. The pub has obviously developed from one terraced house taking in another.

Forester's Arms*, 16 Bank Parade, closed in 1931

These premises were pulled down a number of years ago; the site is now a car park near the old drill hall or former Territorial Barracks. The beerhouse surrendered its license in 1931, one of the last landlords being G. Davey. The sum of £2,081 was paid out in compensation for the premises. Had the premises survived demolition, the fine railed forecourt would have made an excellent beer garden today.

Forgeman's Arms*, 5 Sutcliffe Street, closed in 1934

This beerhouse was unnamed in 1868, though its address is still the same. At this time, it was being run by Lawrence Leach. The Forgeman's Arms used to be located on the corner of Kings Street (now Queens Lancashire Way) and Sutcliffe Street itself, which still survives. The license was one for the sale of beer and lapsed in 1934, when a total of £1,370 was paid in compensation. Mrs M.A. Horner was one of the last licensees. The Forgeman's Arms was formerly the Fireman's Arms. It later became the home of F. Dyson, a loomer, in 1945.

Fox and Pheasant*, 5 Cow Lane, closed in 1958, demolished in 1959

The Fox and Pheasant is an inn that many will recall; it stood in Cow Lane in front of the refurbished lodge building of today. Originally, it was an unnamed beerhouse at No. 5 Cow Lane, run by James Chaddock. It was named the Fox and Pheasant around 1879, when James Chadwick was running the place. He and his wife Anna were still there a couple of years later, when the address was Nos 5 and 7 Cow Lane. There were over a hundred licensed beerhouses during the late 1860s in Burnley. The Fox and Pheasant was one of number of pubs in town owned by William Astley, a Nelson brewery, in the late 1880s. Being one of the nearest pubs to the Empire Theatre and its stage door, it often catered for some of the stage performers there between acts. Its name might well recall the antics of the fox killing the pheasants in the 'Meadows', the old name for this district? Cow Lane is another reminder of the location of the meadows.

The following report appeared in the *Burnley Advertiser*, 1 May 1880:

> Permitting drunkenness. PC Blackburn stated that about 1.30 in the afternoon of the 15th inst, he went to the Fox and Pheasant beerhouse and found the defendant Whittaker drunk. In front of him and close to his right hand was a glass, half full of beer. The defendant afterwards left the house and when witness visited the King's Arms vault, found the defendant sat down again, but was ordered to leave and did so at the bidding of the landlord. Inspector Weir corroborated. James Chadwick said that he was the landlord of the Fox and Pheasant beerhouse, and had been for thirteen years, during which time he had only been brought up once... The landlord was fined 10s and costs, and Whittaker was dismissed.

Free Gardener's*, 31 Mosley Street, closed in 1909

This is the building listed under 'beerhouses' in 1868, when it was run by Henry Astin. He was later running the Park Tavern in 1893. John Blackburn was the landlord at the Free Gardener's in 1879, (see details of the court case below). The license to this beerhouse, now under the GUS and Brun House complex, lapsed in 1909, when a total of £1,900 was paid out in compensation.

One incident involving the landlord of the Free Gardener's is reported in the *Burnley Advertiser*, 19 July 1879:

John Blackburn was summoned for keeping his house open during prohibited hours. John Halstead, Sarah Baron, Sarah Howorth and Sarah Eyron were summoned for aiding and abetting the same. Mr Leresche, barrister at law, defended. PC Blackburn said, 'on Tuesday night, the 8th of the present month, about 8.30 p.m., I was near Blackburn's house, the Free Gardener's Arms, Mosley Street, Burnley. I saw him come from his house and go to another house about three doors away from his house. I remained there from 11.30 to 12.30, suspecting that there was something wrong. At 12.30, he came out of the private house, where I had seen beer on the table, and went into his own house. One of the females came to the door and shouted, 'bring five'. After being in his own house about a minute or two he came out again, and I noticed that he was carrying something. I followed him to the private house, and there found that he had five bottles of beer. I said, 'Blackburn, I thought you would have had more sense. Only up to last week I thought it would have been a caution to you'. He said something about some trouble he had had, and said that he had got nothing for the beer. I told him I should report him for the circumstances. He said, 'you are the same name as myself, and I hope you will not report the matter'.

Defendants Howorth and Eyron both ran upstairs, but eventually, both came down. Susan Baron is the occupier of the house. I had some difficulty in getting out of the house after I said I thought I should report the case. Mr Leresche said that there was no case; no proof of money having been paid, and there was no sale or consumption upon licensed premises at all. The man simply treated the women with some bottled beer, which he had been prevented from selling by the brewery under which the house was held.' The Bench said that they were instructed that the parties had been summoned under the wrong section of the Act, and the case must therefore be dismissed. It is understood however, that the parties will be summoned again under a fresh section.

Friendly Inn, 28 Finsley Gate

There was an unnamed beerhouse of 1868 at No. 26 Finsley Gate, being run by Robert Brunton. It seems more than likely that the inn developed from this, as records show Robert to be running the place in 1879. Robert Brunton later moved on to keep the Finsley Inn, and earlier had kept the Sportsman's Arms on Finsley Gate. Between these two dates, it has been suggested that there were over 500 beerhouses in Burnley, which were then required, by new legislation, to have a name rather than just an address – one landlord named his establishment 'Live and Let Live' and appears to have had an objection to this ruling.

Friendship Inn*, 21 Blackburn Street, closed in 1917

The license of this beerhouse lapsed in 1917 and a total of £2,150 was paid in compensation. Blackburn Street still exists, at least in part, off Brown Street. The inn probably developed out of the unnamed beerhouse of 1868 at No. 19 Blackburn Street, run at this time by William Blakey. This is probably the William Blakey who, in the early 1860s, was listed as a 'tobacco pipe maker' on Blackburn Street. Further evidence of this arrives with the fact that Mrs Alice Blakey was running the beerhouse in 1879 – Alice was a widow two years later and running the beerhouse on her own.

Garrison Hotel, 66 Padiham Road, closed in 1972

Standing side-by-side, guarding the entrance to the old Burnley Barracks, were the Garrison Hotel and the Barracks Tavern at the bottom of Cavalry Street. The Garrison dates from around the 1840s, when, in 1848, Alice Hargreaves was running the inn. By the late 1870s and early 1880s, the Garrison was being run by John and Mary Green, who also had a house servant by the name of Martha Johnson. The Garrison Hotel was advertised for sale in the *Burnley Advertiser*, 4 September 1858:

> To be sold by auction by Messrs Denbigh and Sons at the Cross Keys Inn, Cheapside in Burnley in the County of Lancashire on Monday, 20th day of September 1858 at six o'clock in the evening precisely subject to such conditions as will be there and then produced. All that well accustomed inn or public house called or known by the name of the Garrison Hotel, situated in Habergham Eves with good ale and spirit cellars and an excellent supply of good spring water, stables, backyard and other conveniences belonging therein in the occupation of Richard Salisbury. Also all that messuage or dwelling house adjoining the said public house with cellar, backyard and other conveniences therein the occupation of Mr Flack.

Reports of a court case involving one of the later landlords appears in the *Burnley Advertiser*, 15 December 1877:

> Permitting drunkenness. John Green, landlord of the Garrison Hotel, Padiham Road was charged with supplying drink to a drunken man. Mr W.T. Read, solicitor appeared for the defendant and the officer who proved the case said that on Sunday night at five minutes past nine o'clock, he visited the defendant's house and found a man named William Carnforth there drunk, with a glass of beer in front of him. He spoke to the landlord about it, and he then took it away from him. Mr Read, in defence, said that he should plead guilty to the charge, but urged that the beer had been supplied by his defendant's daughter, who was only nine years of age, and that if the landlord had been present it would not have been supplied. The Bench fined the defendant 40s and costs, the license not to be endorsed.

General Campbell, 20 Barracks Road, closed in 1968

This inn was a little further along the road from the General Havelock. Although both these two houses were named after army leaders of the Indian Mutiny, which took place in 1857-58, the 'General Campbell pub' isn't mentioned in directories until 1868. General Campbell (1792-1863) was a British Field Marshal who commanded the Highland Brigade at Balaclava in the Crimean War, and was Commander-in-Chief during the Indian Mutiny. The General Campbell pub was owned by W. and T. Taylor, an Accrington firm of brewers, in the late 1880s.

General Havelock*, 101 Accrington Road

The 'Havelock' was originally a small beerhouse dating from around 1868, when it was owned by James Mitchell, though it didn't have a name at this time. James Mitchell was still running the place in 1879 when it was selling Massey's ales. The beerhouse was given a full license in

1930, transferred from another pub, the New Sparrow Hawk, which was closed down in that same year. The pub is listed as being at Nos 4 and 6 Barracks Road in the mid-1940s. The landlord at this time was John Wilkinson. Today's regulars might be somewhat surprised to note that the General Havelock is named after a teetotaller. The name of the pub commemorates a British leader in the Indian Mutiny. He commanded the column of men who, in September 1857, effected the relief of Lucknow. Major Henry Sir James Havelock was born in Bishopwearmouth in Sunderland, the second son of Henry Havelock, a well-to-do ship owner. The relief of Lucknow was achieved by Havelock in September 1857, but a second rebel force arrived and besieged the town again – this time it was Havelock and his troops who were trapped inside. It was Sir Colin Campbell – commemorated in the General Campbell pub close by the General Havelock – who was able to relieve Lucknow for the second time in mid-November. However, within days of regaining his freedom, Henry Havelock was dead, overcome by exhaustion and dysentery. He hung on long enough to learn that he had been made a baron, but died before he got word that he had also been promoted to Major General. A public subscription fund raised money to pay for the statue of Havelock which now stands in Trafalgar Square. The plaque beneath reads, 'to Major General Sir Henry Havelock, KCB and his brave companions in arms during the campaign in India 1857. Soldiers, your labours, your privations, your sufferings and your valour, will not be forgotten by a grateful country' – a fitting tribute to a great man. The general was a true teetotaller and temperance-campaigner throughout his life; he even founded a corps for non-drinking soldiers who soon acquired the nickname, 'Havelock's Saints'. On his deathbed, he was heard to remark, 'I die happy and contented' and turning to his son said, 'see how a Christian can die'.

The pub is mentioned in the *Burnley Advertiser*, 1 February 1868:

A violin't assault. John Collinge was summoned for assaulting William M'Donald, an itinerant fiddler. The complainant said that on 20th inst. he went into the Havelock Inn beerhouse, kept by Mr Mitchell in Trinity Street. The defendant and a few others were in the room. While complainant was lighting his pipe, the defendant knocked him down and broke his fiddle. He had not spoken a word to him – he had not played a tune. The defendant knew what he was doing, he was not drunk, but he had had some drink. The fiddle was broken into about fifty pieces. It had cost him 20s, and a gentleman had given it to him about twelve months ago. Defendant to witness: 'Did I strike you?' Witness: 'Yes, you did'. Defendant: 'I have witnesses to prove that I never struck you'. The Bench asked the complainant if he had brought any witnesses. He replied that he was a stranger in town, and could not bring any witnesses, unless the men who were present at the time could be brought. For the defence, Isaac Howarth was called. He stated that he was in the room at the time spoken of by the complainant. The defendant did not strike him, nor break his fiddle. The complainant was getting hold of a glass of beer off the table, and in passing Collinge, he fell against the table and broke his fiddle. He fell with his head against Collinge's legs. The man was drunk. The complainant: 'I was not drunk. I am not in the habit of drinking. The police will be able to tell you whether I was drunk or not'. Mr Alexander said he was not drunk when he came to the station. His fiddle was broken, all in pieces. Complainant to witness excitedly: 'You were stupidly drunk, the other man (the defendant) was not as bad as you, he knew what he was doing'. In answer to the Bench, he said that the fiddle was broken about six o'clock, and he went to the police officer immediately afterwards. The Bench said they could not convict upon the evidence of the complainant unsupported by any witness. They must dismiss the summons.

The Havelock, as it is called by regulars, is named after a teetotaller and British leader in the Indian Mutiny.

General Scarlett, Accrington Road

This pub has opened in the last few years, owned by Moorhouse's – one of Burnley's newest breweries, which is in a handy location for deliveries, directly across the road from the inn. The inn is named after our local hero, the famed General James Yorke Scarlett. James Yorke Scarlett died aged seventy-two in December 1871 and lays buried in a family vault at Cliviger.

General Williams*, Manchester Road

This pub was originally named General Williams, Hero of Kars. In 1879, Henry Edmondson was landlord, but the pub, or beerhouse as it was then, was in existence from at least 1875, (see advert of the beerhouse being offered for sale from the *Burnley Gazette*, 22 May 1875.) The pub is named after Sir William Frederick Williams, born in Nova Scotia, 4 December 1800. During the Crimean War, when the Russians had driven the Turks under the walls of Kars, Colonel Williams, as he was then, was despatched to reorganise the troops. After defending Kars for over four months against the Russians, he met their commander at the head of a large force on the heights above the city and defeated them in a great slaughter of a battle. It was the Sultan of Turkey who conferred the title upon him of the 'Hero of Kars'. He died in London on 26 July 1883. The following advertisement was printed in the *Burnley Gazette*:

Valuable beerhouse and cottages at Roberts' Row near Burnley. To be sold by auction by Mr Denbigh at the Swan Inn, Burnley, on Wednesday, 26 May 1875, at seven o'clock in the evening, in the following or such other lot or lots as may then be decided upon, and subject to conditions to be then produced. Lot 1: All that well accustomed beerhouse called 'General Williams, Hero of Kars' and the two cottages adjoining, situated at and fronting Roberts' Row, Manchester Road, near Burnley, now in the occupation of Mr Henry Edmondson, Alice Roberts, and John Hamilton. Lot 2: All those four cottages, adjoining each other, situated at Roberts' Row aforesaid, (being two at the front and two at the back) with four cellar dwellings under the same, now in the occupation of John Hargreaves, Lavinia Smith, John Thomas Tattersall, Catherine Roberts, Elizabeth Allison, Gabriel Sutcliffe and others. The above premises are situated within a mile of the centre of Burnley, are copyhold of inheritance of the Manor of Ightenhill, and are subject only to nominal copyhold rent. Further particulars may be obtained on application to the auctioneer, 8 Ormerod Street. Mr William Nightingale, agent, 73 Westgate, or at the offices of Messrs Creeke and Sandy, the Solicitors, Burnley.

George IV, 708 Padiham Road, Habergham Eves

This pub was originally named 'the Fighting Cocks', after the 'sport' of that name which doubtless carried on in the vicinity. The pub was one of the few in Burnley that served Dutton's ales – a few of the pub windows for Dutton's ales still survive. William Easton was landlord here at the end of the Second World War. It was at the George and other inns around this part of town in January 1882, that Robert Templeton, a burly Scotsman, went on a drinking spree that was to end in the brutal murder of Betty Scott down Lowerhouse.

Globe Inn*, 47 Bankhouse Street

This Globe Inn closed in 1958 and became a common lodging house for some years afterwards. The pub dates from around 1879 when Ezra Dean was landlord. Another licensee was Harry Harker, who died in January 1939. He kept the house from around 1934 until his death. Harry was a native of Burnley but started out as a weaver at Thornber's Mill – he then went on to open an off-license at No. 16 Rectory Road before going on to become the landlord of the Plane Tree, and finally, the Globe Inn. One of Harry's sons, Willie Harker, at one time played football with Burnley FC. One of the last landlords was Percy Bates who ran the pub in 1945.

Golden Lion, 30/32 Boot Street, closed in 1958

The Golden Lion is yet another Boot Street pub, which was closed down in 1958 and demolished in 1963, for the Pickup Croft development. This beerhouse is listed, though unnamed in 1868, when John Pollard was running it and probably dated from around this time. John Pollard was listed as being a widower by the early 1880s, at which time the inn was still unnamed. In fact, the pub was in the hands of the Pollard family till around 1899. The pub was on the other side of the old Pickup Croft School, separating this and the Devonshire Arms.

This very old photo shows the Gretna in a more placid era; over the door, the sign says that 'billiards' could be played at the inn. (Briercliffe Society)

Great Eastern*, 15 Stanley Street, closed in 1908

The sum of £1,500 was paid out in compensation for this beerhouse (on Stanley Street off Manchester Road) when it was closed down in 1908. The beerhouse was run by the widow, Elizabeth Riley in the early 1880s. She was born in Barnoldswick. The following report of an incident at the Great Eastern appeared in the *Burnley Gazette*, 4 December 1875:

Robert Cottam was charged with being drunk and riotous at the Great Eastern beerhouse, Lane Bridge on Monday night at eight o'clock. He was only a youth. PC 784 said there was a great disturbance in the house; the prisoner had his cap off, and was pulling people about. Lawrence Whittam, the landlord, then preferred a charge of wilful damage against the prisoner. He broke a pane of glass and a picture, and injured the clock, doing damage amounting to 8s. The prisoner appeared to be quite sober. Inspector Weir said the prisoner was drunk when he was brought to the station and in to the cell. Prisoner said he was so drunk he did not know what he was doing. He was fined 10s and costs, or fourteen days for being drunk and riotous, and for the wilful damage he was fined 10s and to pay the damage of 8s, in default fourteen days.

Gretna Green Inn, Coal Clough Lane

The Gretna dates from the mid-1870s and stands at the junction of an ancient highway linking Nick O' Pendle, Ightenhill and Crown Point. Teams of pack horses trod this route laden with salt, limestone and coal in days of yore. On 5 June 1875, the *Burnley Gazette* reports that:

James Noodle was summoned for refusing to quit the Gretna Green public house at half past nine at night on 23 May. He was, at the time, drunk. Mrs McDonna said he went in drunk, kicked up a row and refused to leave when requested. Fined 20s and costs or one month.

The Greyhound was in the middle of a block of properties; to the left was the Black Dog, and to the right was the old Blue Bell Inn. At the time this photo was taken, around 1902, Thomas Ward was landlord. (Briercliffe Society)

Grey Mare Inn, 110 Gannow Lane

In 1848, Thomas Wilkinson was running the Grey Mare. The pub is evidently of great age; the stone-clad roof gives this away, and it seems to stand out architecturally from its surroundings of slate-roofed terraced property. Sadly though, there is no datestone on the building to give the historian a clue as to its age, inspiring a need to delve into the archives for further information. The old inn lacks the grandeur and romance of the old coaching inns and was probably simply built to cater for the needs of canal workers, bargees, or those employed in the cottage industries hereabouts. From the early 1870s, the tavern was taken over by the Moore family who ran the pub for almost forty-five years. This is a feat possibly unequalled by any other family of licensees in town. Many Gannow Lane residents will perhaps recall Dick Greenwood as the landlord of the Grey Mare in the 1960s and 70s.

Greyhound Inn*, 10 Cannon Street, closed in 1907

The Greyhound Inn was down 'Wapping', as that part of town behind the Woolworth car park was called, and its license lapsed in 1907. Joseph Clegg, whose wife died in 1842, kept this beerhouse. Following her death, Clegg sold the place. The new landlord was a Mr Best, a rate collector in town, who leased the building at a rent of seven pounds a year. The Greyhound was a house of apparent ill-repute, and the pub is last mentioned in directories in 1902, when Thomas Ward had the place. In that year, Thomas Ward was charged with three cases of 'harbouring thieves, harbouring women of low character, and permitting drunkenness'. The house was watched from 28 July to 4 August, when a total of fourteen thieves, all of whom had been convicted, were seen to frequent the premises. The landlord submitted in court that he was not aware of the characters of the men and women. The case was dismissed.

Griffin Hotel, Rossendale Road

This inn closed down a few years ago now. It became a health centre, and then (perhaps a little more fittingly, considering that it's directly across from the municipal cemetery) an undertaker's. At the time the Griffin was built (1856), there were no other buildings around it, apart from a few farms, outbuildings, and the cemetery that opened on 1 June 1856. The house was advertised on 4 October 1856, just a few months later. The house was acquired by Grimshaw's from another local brewery, Fernandes, in 1918, but was previously owned by Mr J.T. Dugdale, of Ivy Bank, a cotton manufacturer at the Lowerhouse Mills. The landlord here in 1892 was John Dewhurst, who was convicted of permitting drunkenness on the premises and fined 40s. The Chief Constable objected to the renewing of the license in September of that year, but nevertheless it was granted just the same. From the *Burnley Advertiser*:

> To brewers and Innkeepers: To be let for a term, or from year to year, all that recently erected and commodious inn called 'the Griffin', situated facing the approach to the Burnley Cemetery, in the township of Habergham Eves, together with stables and outbuildings belonging thereto. With the above premises, the tenant may take twelve acres of land adjoining. To view the premises, and to treat for the same, apply to Mr Lawrence Rawcliffe, Lower House.

Grimshaw Arms*, 5 Temple Street, closed in 1911 when £1,600 was paid in compensation

This was originally a beerhouse, though unnamed in 1868. At this time, it was run by Henry Hope, who was mentioned in a court case in 1864. The beerhouse was up for sale by auction which was held at the Thorn Hotel on 13 December 1875 – but few other details were given. The following story is taken from the *Burnley Advertiser*, 9 July 1864:

> James Riley of Crawshawbooth was charged with stealing a suit of clothes belonging to Henry Hope, beer-seller, Grimshaw's Arms, Temple Street Fulledge. The clothes were stolen from the house on 13 February last. The prisoner had lodged there for a short time. The clothes were in the room were he slept on the last night at the house. He was away early in the morning leaving his own clothes and taking Hope's…Committed for trial.

Hall Inn, 2 Church Street, closed in 1963

The Hall Inn was a licensed house with a long history. It was open as early as 1634, when it would have been in competition with the Old Sparrow Hawk for the honour of being the oldest hostelry in the town. It has been suggested that the inn was originally a town house for the Towneley family, but it is more probable that it was used to accommodate overflow guests and servants during the family's periods of entertainment. Like most of the old hotels in town, it formerly had a farm attached. It was rebuilt several times, and in 1716 it was enlarged, with a gallery erected round a courtyard on the Church Street side. Accommodation was available for the travelling public and a bowling green provided relaxation for customers and guests. Around 1740, the property was leased from William Towneley, but the family continued to use the hotel for the Christmas and Easter rent audits, when tenants visited the inn to pay their dues. Free ale, refreshments and tobacco were provided in abundance to sustain the tenants, many of whom had travelled great distances. In the early part of the nineteenth century, the inn was the main theatre in the town and Shakespeare's plays were presented there. As already stated, many attractions were devised during its existence, and, in the course of minor alterations in 1888, a small room was revealed which is believed to have served as a domestic chapel for the Towneley family and guests. Mr J. Grimshaw, of the brewery family, bought the property in 1890 and the house was completely rebuilt in 1907.

One alleged incident at the Hall is recorded in the *Burnley Advertiser*, 24 December 1858:

Mary Ann Roukes charged Sarah Waddington with having assaulted her in the Hall Inn tap on Sunday afternoon the 12th inst. The defendant called two witnesses who were present when the assault was said to have taken place, who stated that nothing had happened. The magistrates dismissed the case.

The Hall Inn is listed under the ownership of Lady O'Hagan in 1888, though it was a free house at the time. Massey's later acquired it, when they took over Grimshaw's in 1928.

On 17 February 1900, the *Burnley Express* refers to the finding of the secret chapel in the Hall by workmen:

Some ten or twelve years ago an interesting discovery was made during some internal alterations at the Hall Inn. Over the assembly room is another small room, which is gained by two or three steps, and the workmen engaged in removing the plaster here found the remains of an old oak-timbered building, which, from its construction, must have stood for centuries. It is well known that this antiquated house is the property of the Towneley family, and it is believed to have once been their town house, and that this room formed the domestic chapel. No doubt the woodwork had been covered over since the last alterations in 1807, referred in the diary thus: 'July 10th, Burnley Fair. Viewed the improvements at the Hall Inn and the new buildings'. Charles Towneley, grandson of John rebuilt almost all of the present front in 1857, as it is to be seen by the inscription on the stonework of one of the windows.

Healey Wood Inn, 26/28 Healey Wood Road, closed in 1972

The Healey Wood Inn probably dates from around 1872 when a John Baxter was running it. An unpretentious little pub which sold 'Astley's ales and stouts', the inn was simply built to cater for the needs of the local population of weavers and miners around the Healey Wood Road area. It was demolished soon after closure in 1972 and there are no remains of the old pub.

Pictorial evidence of the old Grimshaw Arms is rare. This old picture shows the Grimshaw Arms in the middle background, behind the children. Interestingly, the old bollard in the photo still stands near the Oxford Inn on Temple Street.

This photo shows the old Hall Inn at the top of Hall Street before rebuilding. Joseph Brown was the landlord at this time, which dates the image to around 1902. (Briercliffe Society)

This image must date from around 1923 when Willie Astin had the place, as indicated above the doorway. It is probably Willie who we can see in the doorway. But what was the occasion which also brought out his regulars? (Briercliffe Society)

Help Me Through The World, Milton Street

The reader must, by now, appreciate that some Burnley beerhouses had extraordinary names, but surely, 'Help Me Through The World' must be the strangest! The beerhouse was located 'at the bottom of Milton Street', according to a newspaper report. Milton Street ran parallel to Oxford Road, in the area now taken by the Higher and Lower Tentre housing schemes. The landlord's name at the time of the court case in 1867 was John Scholefield. The complicated case was centred around Thomas Hansbrow and Parker Hoyle, who were brought up on remand for breaking into the beerhouse and stealing £9 6s. The case eventually came before a jury, who, after a short consideration, arrived at the verdict of 'not guilty'. The prisoners were then discharged.

Hole in the Wall, 122 Sandygate, closed in 1966

Roger Robinson is one of the first landlords to be mentioned here in 1824 and 1828. This curiously-named inn was demolished to make way for the Trafalgar Flats and was apparently the venue for the last bull-baiting ever to take place in Burnley around 1760. Bear-baiting also took place at the inn. During one performance, the bear escaped and took hold of one the spectators as he struggled frantically to get through a hedge. Happily, he did manage to escape. The inn was frequently the place to be for other sports such as sack races, foot races and donkey races.

The Hole in the Wall public house on Sandygate in 1952. The older inn bore witness to bear-baiting, cockfighting and the Sandygate Races. (Briercliffe Society)

The Sandygate Races were a popular event in times now long-gone. The name is reputed to have come from the fact that one of its first tenants was also a handloom weaver, as was his neighbour. To pass the time of day and indulge in conversation, a hole was knocked through the wall between the two buildings. Another explanation is that the weaver next door could get his beer passed through when the inn was closed and out of hours. This excuse was even used in mitigation in a court case, when the landlord was fined, as reported in the *Burnley Advertiser*, 12 September 1863:

> Breach of the Licensed Victualler Act. William Moorhouse, of the Hole in the Wall public house was summoned for breach of the above Act on the 30 inst. PC Lord said that he visited the house at forty-five minutes past eleven o'clock on the afternoon of the above day. He found four men in the back kitchen and two pint pots, both containing beer. The men were sober. The defendant said that he had only kept the house eleven months, and he was leaving in a few days. Fined 5s and costs.

Hope and Anchor*, 18 Royle Road, closed in 1925

The Hope and Anchor was another beerhouse that had its license lapse in 1924. The place was listed under beerhouses, though not named in 1868, when John Hornby was running it. James Gawthorpe was the landlord here in 1879, and it was named 'Hope and Anchor' in the early 1880s when the landlord was Bolton-born James Logan. His wife, Ellen was working in a cotton mill. A total of £2,200 was paid out in compensation to the last landlord, J. Lord, when it closed down in 1925. The premises were located four or five doors beyond the Salford Hotel, or Town Mouse, in the Stoneyholme direction roughly where the roundabout is today.

Horse and Farrier*, 16 Cannon Street, closed sometime after 1923, when it last appears in the directories

The inn was formerly known as the Blue Bell, and advertised for sale in the Burnley Gazette, 25 April 1874:

> For Sale, the beerhouse known as the 'Farrier's Arms', situated on in Cannon Street in Burnley, aforesaid in the occupation of Robinson Cryer, as tenant thereof, also the cottages or dwelling houses situated at the back of the Farrier's Arms with garden and conveniences respectively belonging to.

This beerhouse became the 'Horse and Farrier' around 1879 when Michael Gaynor was running the inn. The inn was down 'Wapping', a notorious area of low-class dwelling, lodgings, houses, and inferior inns. The place is now taken by the Woolworth's car park, and is allegedly nicknamed after 'Moll of Wapping'. In August 1902, the landlady here, a Mrs Pawson, was charged under the Licensing Act of 1872, which read that 'loose women should not be allowed to remain on licensed premises longer than was necessary for the obtaining of reasonable refreshment'. Some women, it was stated, had gone into the house several times a day in the company of men, and several of them stayed there two hours or longer. The Bench said that Mrs Pawson was aware of the character of the people who visited her house, and she was fined £10 and costs. However, her license would not be endorsed.

The inn features in the *Burnley Gazette*, 30 January 1875:

> Joseph Roberts and William Sullivan, neither of whom appeared were charged with disorderly conduct by fighting in the front room of the Horse and Farrier beerhouse, Cannon Street. On Saturday night, PC Briggs was sent for to part them, which he did; they were both sober. Both defendants have made repeated visits to the courthouse on various charges. The Bench fined them 20s and costs, or one month in default.

Inkerman Inn*, 234/236 Accrington Road, closed in December 1950

This inn, formerly a beerhouse, was located on the corner of Accrington Road and Hartley Street, directly across from the Alma Inn. The name is associated with the Battle of Inkerman that took place in the Crimean War on 5 November 1854. It was still listed under 'beerhouses' in 1937, when Sam Barlow was running the place, though by 1945 it is listed under 'Hotels and Inns'. Sam was still running the inn at this time. Following the closure of the inn, the building was used for a time as flats. The site today is taken by the garage forecourt. Landlord here in 1892 was Eli Dewhurst who was fined on 30 March that year for permitting drunkenness. When his license came up for renewal in September that year, the Chief Constable objected, but it was renewed nevertheless with a warning over future behaviour. Eli also stated that his beerhouse was licensed before 1869, and probably dated from around that time.

Jolly Collier's, Rossendale Road

This beerhouse is marked on the 1844 map and was near the junction with Cog Lane. Little doubt, the many colliers who lived in this area of Back Lane would be 'jolly' after a night out in the beerhouse. It may have been that the colliers were actually paid at the inn – a practice not uncommon. The Jolly Collier's is not mentioned in any directories, though it may have been the house of Thomas Maden, farm labourer and beer-seller, who appears in the 1851 census.

Jolly Sailor, 'near Rodney Street'

This beerhouse was on the site of the Old Market Hall, which opened in 1871, and described as being 'near Rodney Street'. Mary Wood, a Bradford lass kept the place at one time; it was she who gave a 'performance' of walking 1,000 miles in 1,000 hours, at Glen View in November 1864. By December, nearly 3,000 spectators had been to see her walk. A strange name for an inland pub!

Junction Hotel, 63 Rosegrove Lane

Originally, the 'Junction Inn', this establishment dates from around 1872, when James Haworth was running the inn. All the hostelries in Rosegrove have links with the railway, which is apt, for the 'village' grew up around the Rosegrove sidings and railway. The Junction in the late 1880s was owned by Shaw and Co., a Blackburn brewery.

King's Arms, 5 Bridge Street

There was a beerhouse listed at No. 7 Mill Lane (the old name for Bridge Street) in 1868, being run by George Wood. It seems more than likely that the two premises were knocked through to give larger accommodation at some time. The King's Arms probably dates from around the 1840s and by 1848 Joseph Varley is listed as landlord here. In the 1880s, John Ingham was the innkeeper. On 24 January 1863, the Burnley Advertiser reports how:

> Thomas Parker, a bully, and Ann Smith, a prostitute, were charged with violent assault on Thomas Heaton in the King's Arms tap on Saturday last. They were fined 20s and costs, and in default were committed to one month in the House of Correction.

Lamb Inn*, 33 Red Lion street, closed in 1958 with the redevelopment of the Croft Street area

John Smith was running the Lamb in 1879 when it was listed as a beerhouse. The inn, however, predates this time. Charles Wells kept the Lamb Inn just after the war when it was located next to the former Enon Baptist chapel near the bottom of the bus station.

The Junction in Rosegrove, like many other inns, has evolved from one old cottage which expanded to take in others.

Lancashire and Yorkshire*, 9 Padiham Road, closed in 1955

The Lancashire and Yorkshire pub was the very last house on what remains of the old Padiham Road, overlooking the Barracks Station. The inn, originally a beerhouse, takes its name from the Lancashire and Yorkshire Railway Company, the lines of which ran alongside the pub. One of the last landlords would have been Giles Pickles who kept the pub in 1947. On 25 January 1868, the *Burnley Advertiser* reports that:

> Henry Hartley, landlord of the Lancashire and Yorkshire Hotel, Westgate, Burnley was summoned for a breach of the Licensing Act on the 12th inst. at about thirty-five minutes past ten o'clock in the morning. PC Lord said that he visited the defendant's house, and found a man sitting in the kitchen with a glass of beer before him. He went into the front room first, but saw the man in passing the kitchen. When he went into the kitchen, the landlady was putting the glass of beer into the cupboard... There having been no previous complaints against the house, the magistrates fined the defendant 5s and costs, in default seven days.

Lane Ends, Kiddrow Lane

Look for the entwined initials of Massey's Burnley Brewery carved in the stonework, and the owl, the symbol of Massey's Brewery. Before being rebuilt shortly after 1926, the Lanes Ends was the later name for the Bird in Hand.

Lifeboat Inn, 6 Parker Lane

The Lifeboat Inn would have been around where the army surplus store is today on Parker Lane. It didn't have a long existence, from around 1868, when it was listed without a name, simply under 'beerhouses', and run by Nancy Baxter, to 1888. It is also listed as being owned by Alexander Bell, a Barrowford brewery. After this, it changed its name to the Marlborough. Sandy McLintock, a popular captain of Burnley Football Club, became the landlord of the Marlborough on his retirement from the game. Strange name for a pub, considering we are some forty-odd miles from the sea! George Sykes ran the inn during the early to mid-1870s, and was prosecuted on a number of times for breach of the licensing laws. This extract from the *Burnley Gazette*, 10 February 1872, reports that:

> George Sykes, of the Lifeboat beerhouse, Parker Lane was summoned for having music and dancing without a license. Mr Nowell appeared for the defendant, and Mr Creeke watched the case on behalf of the police. PS Rainey stated that on the 26th inst. at twenty minutes to ten o'clock, he visited the house of the defendant. He found there a man playing a fiddle, and some men dancing. He asked the defendant if he knew what was being done was an offence, and he assented, but said he did not see much harm in it. The men were step dancing, one after another. Mr Nowell called the man who was playing, named Cudworth, and the two men who were dancing, to show that the fiddler was not employed by the defendant, but had gone there of his own accord, and had been asked by the other witnesses to play for them… The Bench took this view of the case, and fined the defendant 2s 6d and costs and refused to admit the prisoners to bail.

The Lifeboat is also mentioned in the *Burnley Advertiser*, 29 December 1877:

> Swamped in the Lifeboat. Robert Wilson was charged with permitting drunkenness at the Lifeboat Inn, Burnley on the 15th inst, and Robert and John Pollard with being accessories thereto. The case engaged the Bench for a long time and in it, so much conflicting testimony was given, which drew the remark from one or more members of the Bench that perjury existed on one hand or the other. The magistrates decided that the offence had been proved against the Pollards. They were fined 10s each and costs, or fourteen days. Against Wilson, they considered that there was not sufficient evidence to convict.

Little White Horse, See New White Horse

Loose Pulley, Robert's Row

Robert's Row was off Manchester Road, but little else is known about this beerhouse, other than the drinking charge brought before the landlord in 1858, as documented by the *Burnley Advertiser*, on 22 May:

> Edward Pollard of the Loose Pulley beerhouse, Robert's Row was charged with having a number of men drinking in his house at five minutes past ten on Friday the 7th inst., four of whom were stripped and fighting. The defendant said the men were not fighting, and although

it was not time to turn out, he did turn the men out at the order of the policeman. A witness called by the defendant said that the men were not drunk. He called a man drunk when he could not walk straight. He had gone to the Loose Pulley between then and four o'clock in the afternoon with four others. They went in just as they had come from work, and being a finishing afternoon they were in their shirt sleeves. The rest went about seven o'clock. They clubbed what money they had for the drink they got, and then went on the 'tick'. There was no attempt at fighting. Fined 10s and costs.

Lord Nelson*, 39 Bridge Street, closed in 1908

The license to this beerhouse lapsed in 1908, and a sum of £756 was paid out in compensation. The Lord Nelson was just before the junction with Bank Parade on Bridge Street. The place was owned by Alexander Bell of the Clough Springs Brewery at Barrowford in the 1880s. Thomas Kennedy was landlord here from 1879 to 1883; he was born in Hull. His wife was Irish-born Catherine, and the beerhouse supplemented its income by taking in a few lodgers. Probably the last landlord was Michael Gallagher.

Malakoff Tavern*, 50 Trafalgar Street, closed in 1966

This tavern is named after a Russian Fort, which stood near Sebastopol during the Crimean War. The constable in the court case below appears to have had a remarkable sense of hearing, according to this account taken from the *Burnley Advertiser*, 30 November 1861;

Heaton Atkinson, beer-seller, Malakoff Inn Trafalgar Street was summoned for permitting gaming in his house on Sunday night, 16th inst. The constable said that about 8.00 p.m. that night while outside he heard that they were playing cards inside. He heard money being exchanged and cards dealt and played. The door was fast so he could not get in; he waited a short time and a man came out, he then rushed in and found three or four men playing and others looking on. The landlord was present looking over. There was money on the table, and he got the cards. Fined £1 10s and costs.

Mason's Arms, 60 St James's Street, closed in 1958

This inn was evidently of some antiquity, although it was rebuilt. In 1824, it is listed under the name of Elizabeth Eastwood, but by 1848, Sarah Allen was running the inn. Three generations of the Allen family ran the pub: grandfather, son and grandson. The Mason's Arms is mentioned in the *Burnley Advertiser*, 22 May 1858:

Henry Blakey, alias 'Plucks', was charged with stealing six half-crowns from the person of Robert Sumner. It appeared that the prisoner and the prosecutor had been drinking together in the Mason's Arms on Monday evening. Sumner treated the prisoner with both ale and spirits, Sumner got up and went to the door, and he was quickly followed by the prisoner. When in the doorway, the prisoner seized Sumner and slipped his hands into his side pocket. They then both went out, Blakey returned to the tap before Sumner. When Sumner returned, he charged the prisoner with having taken his money, and then Blakey threw down a half-crown and left the tap. Martha Stowell, the keeper of the tap, said that she saw the prisoner put his hand in Sumner's pocket, and after pulling it out, he put his hand in his own pocket. She told the prisoner to deliver up the money he had got. After leaving the tap, the prisoner returned and asked her to fill him a glass of brandy. She refused, and said she would not fill him any more for other people's money. She gave the information to the police. The prisoner was apprehended a little before twelve o'clock the same night at the Market Tavern by Police Constable Wildman. He made no reply to the charge, and when searched he had no money on him. Committed for trial.

The name of the Mason's Arms appears again in the *Burnley Gazette*, 22 June 1878:

William Crossley was charged with having stolen a barrel from the yard of Mr John Allen, of the Mason's Arms on the 8 June, and George Whittaker with having received the same, knowing it to be stolen. Prosecutor said he missed the barrel from his yard between the hours of ten and eleven in the morning on the day in question. Albert Howarth said that he saw the prisoner get the barrel out of the yard and roll it down the street. He asked leave of the witness to borrow a truck to take it away, but he refused. He eventually took the truck belonging to Mr James Thompson. Witness heard the prisoner ask a man if he wanted to buy a barrel, but the person said that he did not want one. PS Bland spoke of apprehending the prisoner the same afternoon in the Market Place, and charged him with stealing the barrel from the backyard of the Mason's Arms. He replied, 'all right'. About ten o'clock on Tuesday night, he went to Whittaker's house and asked him where the porter cask was that he had bought off Crossley. He denied buying one, and also denied seeing one. Witness told him he knew that he had bought the barrel, so that he had better admit it, and he further denied any knowledge of it. On searching the house he found the barrel (produced) in a coal cellar adjacent to the house, partly covered in coals and boxes... Both prisoners pleaded guilty and were committed to the sessions for trial.

Meadow's Inn*, 2 King Street, closed in 1959

The Meadow's Inn is suitably named, for this area of land was once all meadows, as testified by Cow Lane that leads onto it. The pub dates from around 1879, when Abraham Crabtree was running it. In 1871, the landlord and landlady here were Jonathan and Mary Preston. I believe that the inn became a lodging house for some years after its closure.

Mechanic's Arms*, 8 Finsley Gate, closed in 1916

License for this beerhouse lapsed in 1916, when £1,500 was paid in compensation – it later became R. Silcock and Sons oil cake manufacturers. The Mechanic's Arms, as an unnamed beerhouse back in the early 1880s, was run by Alf Sterling, 'beerhouse keeper'.

Miller's Arms, 20 Junction Street, closed in 1978

This is probably the unnamed beerhouse on Junction Street in 1868, which at this time, was being run by Henry Hartley. The pub took its name from the nearby Junction Street Mill,

The old Mason's Arms was the home of three generations of the Allen Family. (Briercliffe Society)

formerly a corn mill, though later the Economics. The pub is named as the Miller's Arms in the early 1880s when it was being run by Henry and Rebecca Hartley.

Miller's Arms*, 34 Parker Street, closed in 1956

This inn was on the other corner of Yarm Place, which still exists between Standish Street and the car park of the former GUS Building. In 1923, the inn was run by J. Byrne. In a directory printed in 1945, the pub is noted as being the Miller's Tavern and was run by Mrs Marian Culpan. The *Burnley Express* mentions one incident at the Miller's on 24 August 1878:

Henry Hartley, landlord of the Miller's Arms beerhouse was summoned for a breach of the Licensing Act by keeping the house open for the sale of intoxicating liquor during prohibited hours. Edward Campbell and Joseph Whittaker were charged with being unlawfully on licensed premises. PC Lawson said that 'at half past eight o'clock on Sunday morning the 4th inst., I was on duty on Parker Street close to the Miller's Arms beerhouse kept by Hartley. I saw two men come out of the side door. Soon afterwards, three more went to the side, one entered and the other gave a bottle to the landlord. I saw the first man who had entered drink a glass of beer. He came out again, and the other man who had given Hartley the bottle entered. I then went across the road and met the man who came out first. Shaking some money in my pocket I said "I wonder if there is any chance of having a glass of beer". He said "Oh yes, plenty". I went into the house and met Hartley with a large jar in his hand at the door containing half a gallon of beer. I saw a man sitting in the house at a table by the name of Edward Campbell, with a glass before him. I had seen him drink the ale before getting into the room. Defendant Whittaker was standing in the passage. Mrs Hartley made the remark when I got into the kitchen, "we shall be caught, that will be about it". I said, "I believe you will". I then had the jar in my hand which I had taken from Hartley... 'The Bench fined the landlord 20s and costs, but did not endorse the license. The other defendants were fined 10s and costs.

Miller's Arms Pilling Street, closed

Possibly this is the unnamed beerhouse mentioned in a directory of 1868, at No. 1, Pilling Street when it was being run by William Wilson. Pilling Street was off Norton Street that was in Pickup Croft. There used to be Pillingfield Mill, a corn mill on Aqueduct Street, (now part of Centenary Way) – no doubt the millers who worked there used the pub.

Mitre Inn, 120 Westgate closed in 1998, license lapsed in 2002

We are told that the Mitre Hotel was built by Mr Ward, the agent for Mr Towneley Parker of Cuerden, and who dwelt at Springwood, in *Reminiscences of Old Burnley,* a series of articles in the *Burnley Express* in 1899. However, the exact year it was built is not mentioned. Edward and Esther Griffiths were running the Mitre in 1871, although the inn was being run under tenancy of Samuel Holt when it was to be sold at auction on the 14 June 1875 (see advertisement below, taken from the *Burnley Gazette,* 29 May 1875). At this time, the inn was tied to the Nelson brewery of Brown and Astley. In more recent years, the pub was in the news when the body of a newborn child was found tucked away in newspaper in a chimney breast in one of the upper bedrooms at the inn. The identity of the child or its mother was never discovered – however, the body of the poor infant was given a decent burial courtesy of a local undertaker. The following advertisement was printed in the *Burnley Gazette*:

Valuable public house for sale within the Borough of Burnley. To be sold by auction, by Messrs M. and T. Watson, at the house of Mr Samuel Holt, the Mitre Inn, Burnley, on Monday, the fourteenth day of June next, at three o'clock in the afternoon subject to such conditions as shall be then and there produced, all that commodious and well accustomed inn or public house situated in Westgate, Burnley, at its junction with Trafalgar Road and Trinity Street, called 'the Mitre Inn' now in the occupation of Mr Samuel Holt as tenant thereof, together

A view of the old Mitre Inn looking along towards Trafalgar Street. Notice F. Groome's garage on the corner of Westgate and Trafalgar Street. (Briercliffe Society)

with the yard, wash-house, and appurtenances thereto belonging, also all that four-stalled stable and coach-house with hayloft over, together with all that three-stalled stable adjoining, and also that cottage site in and being No. 1 Cranmer Street, also that cottage situated over the coach house, and which is now unoccupied. The hotel contains in the basement very extensive wine, spirits and beer cellars with stone-vaulted roofs, on the ground floor Commercial room, parlour, bar, bar parlour, vault, kitchen, scullery, pantry and spacious corridors; on the first floor a well furnished billiard room, 38 feet 6 inch by 16 feet, sitting room and four bedrooms; on the second floor, three bedrooms and clubroom, and bathroom, the latter being fitted up with hot and cold water. The whole of the premises are in excellent repair, neatly and substantially stone-built, being well-furnished throughout, and have a building frontage to Cranmer Street of 79 feet, Trafalgar Road of 43 feet, and to Westgate of 42 feet. The Mitre Inn being situated at the junction of three of the best and most frequent thoroughfares in Burnley, and within 100 yards of the Burnley Barracks Station of the Lancashire and Yorkshire Railway, its situation is daily improving in value. The property is of freehold tenure, and will be sold subject to the payment of yearly ground rent of 12s and to a lease thereof to Messrs Brown and Astley, and which expires in the month of March 1876. The tenant will show the premises, and further information may be had on application to Mr Humphrey Bracewell, the owner, Westgate, Burnley, to the auctioneers at their office, 58 Manchester Road, Burnley, and at the offices of Messrs Artindale and Artindale, the solicitors, Burnley.

Today, the Mitre Inn still stands, but it is in a dilapidated condition and it seems doubtful that it will ever again be a public house. Many though will remember happier times at the inn when you had to queue to get a game of dominoes or cards on a Sunday dinnertime. And how many regulars remember Ernie Hutchies' donkey in the stable in the backyard of the inn, I wonder?

Today this inn is named the Ministry of Ale, but was originally called the Lord Nelson Inn.

Nelson Hotel, 9 Trafalgar Street, closed in 1998, but reopened as Ministry of Ale

The pub was originally named the Lord Nelson Inn, taking its name, of course, from the famed admiral. One of the early records of the pub is in 1868, when T. Sutcliffe was running the place. By 1871, it had been taken over by Catherine Sutcliffe, and her three children, Alice, Richard and Mary. At the time of writing, the inn had reopened under another name – the Ministry of Ale. One incident connected to the Nelson Hotel was reported in the *Burnley Advertiser*, 10 January 1863:

Stealing brushes. Margaret Haworth, a married woman, was charged with stealing two brushes – the property of James Rawlinson, a brush and fancy goods hawker, Burnley Lane, on 2nd inst. The prosecutor stated that he was hawking his wares on the 2nd inst. and called at the Nelson Hotel, Trafalgar Street. The prisoner was in the house, and the prosecutor and another man went into the room where she was. There was another woman in the room where she was besides the prisoner. They were drinking a quart of ale. They stayed there about an hour and a half, but during that time he had occasion to go out. He had the goods in his basket covered up. He noticed that the basket appeared as if someone had put their hands in. He called the landlord and landlady, and said to them, 'I think someone has been in my basket that had no business'. They then told him to look in his basket and see if anything had been taken out. He did so, but could not tell them at the time what had been taken.

Was the old Neptune Inn on Sandygate so named on account of the bargees from the Leeds and Liverpool Canal regularly using the inn, I wonder?

He left the house and called at the Canal Tavern, he found that two scrubbing brushes had been taken. The value of the brushes was 2s 3d. He went back to the Nelson Hotel, but the landlord did not know anything about them. He told him to go to Miss Green's beerhouse and see there. He went there and spoke to Miss Green about the brushes. She said the prisoner had just been and left one. She gave him the brush... The Bench said they thought it doubtful that the brushes had been taken with felonious intent, and therefore they would dismiss the case. At the same time they recommended her to leave off drinking, and advised her to stay at home more with her husband.

Neptune Inn, 29 Sandygate, closed in 1914

The Neptune always remained in the same location and was marked on the map of 1851. The name is a suitable one for an inn frequented by bargees and other workers on the canal, just up the road. James Heap was running the inn, according to a directory in 1848. The landlord here in 1871 was William Kay, ably assisted by his wife, Elizabeth, and daughter, ten-year-old Matilda. The longest-serving landlord at the Neptune was John Witham, from 1899 to its closure. The modest inn continued its trade until 1914, when its full license was transferred to the newly opened Rose and Crown, Manchester Road. For many years, the premises were used as a working men's club, the Transport Union Offices and, if verbal evidence is anything to go on, as John Watts's canteen. The more observant passer-by might just notice that the 'hook' over the cellar drop still remains on Neptune Street.

New Albion, Rossendale Road

The name changed to the Running Pump in later years. Since this time, the pub closed down, and is now a restaurant. The 'new' pub opened its doors, just a few days before Christmas in 1939, with the transferring of the license from the 'old' Albion on Red Lion Street to here, as the 'New Albion'. The pub, built by Massey's, was described as 'one of the most up to date premises to be found for many miles around Burnley'. There was also ample lavatory accommodation for both sexes, it was stated. One of the first, if not the first, landlord was Arthur Fryer.

New Hotel, 20 Cog Lane, closed in 1978

'Paddy' McGinty, who later took on the Peels Arms on Padiham Road, kept this cosy little pub on Cog Lane near its junction with Gannow Lane for a number of years. John Fletcher kept the New Hotel back in the mid-1940s.

New Market Hotel, 25 Market Street, closed in 1962

This house stood on the site of Swallow Hall, built in the late eighteenth century by William Crook. It had extensive gardens at the front and at the rear was a brewhouse with more land extending to the river. With the rapid growth of the town and the transfer of the market from Manchester Road and St James's Street, the hall was converted to a licensed house, with Thomas Howard as the landlord of what was then the New Market Hotel. Prior to 1850, a music hall was added to the comforts and, as an enticement to patrons to sample its delights, a pint of ale was included in the admission charge. It was completely gutted by fire in 1888. However, restoration took place, but with strong competition coming from other theatres being set up in the town its popularity gradually declined. The following advert appeared in the *Burnley Advertiser*, February 1858:

> Reopening of the Market Tavern concert room. T. Duckworth begs to inform his friends and the public that he will be opening the above room on Monday, 7 February 1853 when the following distinguished talent will appear: Mrs Reeves, the pleasing ballad singer, Mr Reeve, the celebrated comic singer, Mr Lawrence... comic singer, and Mr E. Llewellyn, sentimental vocalist.

The pub is mentioned a second time in the *Advertiser* on 20 December 1862:

> Robert King, a stripper and grinder, was summoned for assaulting Anthony Flynn, a labourer. The complainant said that on Saturday night week, he and some companions went to the Market Tavern. While drinking their ale, some [entertainers] were amusing the company. He and the others laughed at their performance, when King got up and asked him what he was laughing at him for. Complainant denied he was laughing at him. King then kicked the complainant, who immediately made another stroke back. Upon this King knocked the complainant down, inflicting a cut on his forehead. The Bench fined King, who did not appear, 10s and costs, in default fourteen days' imprisonment.

In the late 1920s regular boxing shows were held in the Market Tavern and some prominent exponents appeared there, including Jock McAvoy, the British and European middleweight champion. Later the upstairs room served as the headquarters of the Burnley Garrick Club under the name of the Phoenix Theatre. The New Market Hotel was among the properties that were demolished in 1962 to make way for the present market complex.

New Red Lion, 13 Manchester Road, open at time of writing as Big Window

This pub will be remembered by many as the 'big window' and served for a time as Murphy's. The New Red Lion (another of the pub's previous names) was a Dutton's house – one of a few in Burnley back in 1888. The pub has, of course, big windows, but some argue that the windows of the 'Little' White Horse (New White Horse) on Hammerton Street were bigger!

The pub is mentioned in the *Burnley Advertiser*, 9 July 1864:

George Woods Stones of the New Red Lion was summoned for having his chimney on fire the previous Thursday. Mr Slater stated that he had seen the chimney on fire. He went in and found an old basket on the fire. On asking why this had been placed there, he was told by the wife of the defendant that it had been done to make the oven draw. Defendant said that he was away from home at the time, and was not aware of what had been done. He was generally most careful as he had so much straw and hay on the premises. Fined 5s and costs.

New Sparrow Hawk, 82/84 Church Street, closed in 1930

The license for this pub lapsed in 1930. The inn was located on Church Street, but on the opposite side to the Old Sparrow Hawk. The New Sparrow Hawk was, at one time, also home to the village 'bobby' William Chaffer. Old 'Chaffer' the constable was described as deputy constable and landlord of the New Sparrow Hawk and was, for a long time, a familiar figure in the town. On one occasion, a special body of watchmen was formed to guard the sleeping town. They used to go the rounds and call out the hour, adding remarks about the weather. Sentry boxes were stationed at various intervals for protection in inclement weather. October 1906 saw the death of Sophia Parker who kept the inn from around 1879 up until her retirement in 1904. Sophia was born at Lee Green Farm at Extwistle in 1822. Sophia married Mr Daniel Parker in 1844 and for some years lived at Holden Farm, Extwistle. She took over as landlady of the New Sparrow Hawk in the late 1870s following the death of Daniel. Daniel Parker is, in fact, mentioned in a court case of 1868.

Recorded in the *Burnley Advertiser* is one instance when he was summoned to court on the 11 January 1868:

Daniel Parker, landlord of the New Sparrow Hawk Inn, Church Street was summoned for a breach of the Licensing Act on Sunday 29th inst. Defendant did not appear, but his son was in court. PC Lord said that at half past three o'clock on the afternoon named he visited the defendant's house. On entering the door, the landlady ran into the bar with something under her apron – a pint jug containing whiskey... Fined 10s and costs.

The 'big window' pub on Manchester Road was formerly known as the New Red Lion.

New White Horse*, 18 Hammerton Street

Known as the Little White Horse to many, this place was originally built as a private house in 1850. It became a pub in 1869, and in the year 1879, Thomas Rawstron was running the place. He features in the following article from the *Burnley Advertiser*, 10 April 1880:

> At the Preston Sessions on Thursday, a case of appeal of some importance was heard before W.H. Higgin and other magistrates. The appellant was Thomas Rawstron of the New White Hart Inn, Burnley, beer-seller, and the respondents were Superintendent Wright and the borough magistrates. Mr Shee, instructed by Mr Hodgson, solicitor, Burnley appeared for the defendant, Thomas Rawstron. The appeal arose under the following circumstances; on the 24 December last, Rawstron was summoned before the borough magistrates charged with permitting drunkenness at his house on 13 December last. PS Parker gave evidence before the magistrates. There was no evidence to show that Hartley went into the house, or that any beer had been supplied to him by Rawstron and under the circumstances the court was of the opinion that the conviction must be quashed.

It appears that Thomas Rawstron did not stay in the licensed trade, for the following year he had moved back to his mother's house at 5 Lindsay Street and had taken work as a cotton weaver.

Oddfellow's Tavern*, 18 Boot Street, or Croft Street?

Also known as the Oddfellow's Arms, this beerhouse surrendered its license in 1907. Thomas Greenwood, who also worked as an engine driver, opened the place after leaving the Blue Bell, down Wapping. The beerhouse is unnamed in a directory of 1868, though the address is the same, and Thomas Greenwood was still running it. He is mentioned in connection with a court case in the *Burnley Advertiser*, 12 September 1863:

> Breach of Beer Act. Thomas Greenwood, Oddfellows Arms, Croft Street was summoned for a breach of the act on 30th inst. PC Lord said that he visited the house at fifty minutes past three o'clock in the afternoon, and found three men and a woman in the house, and a pint jug of ale put in the cupboard. Fined 5s and costs.

In later years, around 1923, the premises became J. Wadsworth's hairdressers. The beerhouse was just beyond the Baptist chapel towards the bus station.

Old Duke*, 6 Briercliffe Road

The name of the pub is a reference to the Duke of Wellington, Arthur Wellesley (1769-1852), the commander in the Peninsular War. Robert Thornber was one of the earliest landlords here in 1879.

Old House at Home*, 166 Sandygate, closed in 1964

I offer no explanation for the curious naming of this cosy little pub located on the old part of Sandygate, now named Burnham Gate. The inn was an unnamed beerhouse back in the early 1880s when the landlord was Septimus Fishwick; his wife helped out around the place. John Lord was landlord here in the 1920s, and Mrs Mary Fowler in 1945.

Old Red Lion, 4 Manchester Road

The history of the Old Red Lion house dates back to the seventeenth century when the Ingham family of Fulledge House was prominent in the area. It was from the Inghams, in the early eighteenth century, that Henry Blackmore, a local colliery owner, purchased the Red Lion Crofts, which included the Red Lion with its brewhouse, shippon and stables. The landlord most closely associated with the Old Red Lion was probably James Pate, a stage coach driver, who used the house as a centre for his coaching activities, driving his six-horse stage to Manchester on Mondays and Thursdays and returning the following day. During the tenancy of the Pate family the following sign was displayed inside the inn: 'Thou mortal man that lives on bread, what makes thy face to look so red? Thou silly fop that looks so pale, it's red with supping Jim Pate's ale'.

In addition to the landlord's coaching activities, other carriers used the inn's stabling facilities, with a regular service to Colne departing at 9 a.m. during the week and 10 a.m. on Sundays. In 1865, the newly formed Burnley Council bought the inn and actually had it demolished. At the time, it was a suggested site for the new town hall, but the proposal was vetoed with the result that in 1868, the hotel was rebuilt on its present site, coinciding with the widening of Manchester Road.

The Old Duke Inn near Duke Bar is named, like a number of others in town, after the Duke of Wellington.

The Old Red Lion before being rebuilt was a ramshackle affair, converted from a number of lowly old cottages. (Briercliffe Society)

The Old Red Lion was put up for sale by auction on 28 August 1851, when the inn was described as:

Lot 10: All that capital messuage inn and public house called the Old Red Lion Inn, with the shop front, carriages houses, stables, buildings, yard and premises thereto (being one of the chief inns and corner premises) fronting on to the Market Place and Market Street respectively in Burnley, partly adjoining Lots 8, 9, 11 and 12 and the intended court or passage from Red Lion Street aforesaid. Tenant, Adam Robinson innkeeper and under tenants.

The pub in the 1880s was, as it is now, a Thwaites' house and rated at £243 10d, holding a publican license – the landlord and landlady at this time were William and Maria Bancroft.

Old Sparrow Hawk, 65 Church Street

There has been a Sparrow Hawk almost as long as there has been the town of Burnley, although it has been rebuilt, of course. Sarah Hind, whose name appears over the doorway in a number of photographs of the inn, was the widow of Shuttleworth Hind, who died in 1893. A drinking tankard with Shuttleworth's name on it was found a number of years ago. Interestingly, the pub, a free house, was owned by Lady O'Hagan in the 1880s and was, for a long time, in the hands of the Towneleys. John Towneley, in fact, bought the property and land in 1586, when the inn was established under the name of the Old Sparrow Hawk. The Towneley family crest features a sparrow hawk. The inn remained in the possession of the family for many years and at one time was referred to as 'Church Inn', due to its association with St Peter's church across the street. The old inn was a prominent feature at 'top o' town' until 1896, when the present building, designed by a rising young local architect named Charles Parsons, was integrated into the new Ormerod Road property complex (then in the course of being erected). In 1953, 'the Sparrow' boasted that 'it was appointed by the RAC and the AA', offering 'excellent cuisine, well-appointed spacious lounges, and dinning rooms, wedding or dinner parties a speciality' with Miss F.M. Cowgill as the manageress. Since that time, adjoining property has been acquired and added to the Sparrow and a major facelift in 1965 gave the hotel a still more attractive appearance. Today it is one of, if not the finest hotel in the borough.

One court case concerning Shuttleworth Hind is recorded in the *Burnley Gazette*, 19 April 1873:

Shuttleworth Hind, keeper of the Old Sparrow Hawk, was summoned for breach of his license by having the house open during prohibited hours on Sunday the 6th inst. Elizabeth Smith was summoned for being on the premises for unlawful purposes. PC Pierce saw Smith come out of the house carrying something, and followed her to her home where there were three men and two women. She refused to let him look at what she had got and poured it down the slopstone. He examined the jug and found a small quantity of beer and foam at the bottom...The Bench said that if the man had been in Hind's house, it might have been a different thing. Hind was fined 20s and costs and Smith 1s and costs, or seven days. License not to be endorsed.

Old Wheatsheaf*, 112 Colne Road

Known simply as the 'Wheatsheaf' now that the original Wheatsheaf has gone from Croft Street in the town centre, this inn on Colne Road dates from around 1879, when Isaac Ashworth

Before the inn was rebuilt in 1868, the site was considered for use as the town hall. The present-day Old Red Lion dates from this era. (Briercliffe Society)

This photo of the Old Sparrow Hawk dates from 1887, not long before the inn was rebuilt, when the landlord here was Lawrence Witham. (Briercliffe Society)

Left: The Wheatsheaf on Colne Road was originally named the 'Old Wheatsheaf' to distinguish it from the Wheatsheaf which used to be on Croft Street in the town centre.

Opposite: You might expect the Oxford pub to be on Oxford Road, but its address is Temple Street!

was running the place. In 1888, the inn was in private hands, belonging to James Hey (also the landlord of the Prince of Wales) but was tied to Grimshaw's ales.

Owl in the Wood*, 3 Springfield Road, closed in 1974

This was originally an unnamed beerhouse listed in a directory of 1868 at No. 3, Springfield Road, when it was being run by John Woabank. Henry Chambers was running it by 1879.

Oxford Inn*, 1 Temple Street

The Oxford Inn was originally a beerhouse dating from around 1868. Though still unnamed at this time, its address is the same and the house was being run by Robert Roberts. By the early 1880s, the inn was run by William and Mary Hargreaves. They were helped out by a young servant lass, Elizabeth Halton. The inn sign of today shows a Morris Oxford car, but surely, the place is named after the university and the boat race. After all, there was a Cambridge Inn just around the corner. Walter Pickard, son of the landlord at the Oxford Inn, was killed on the 21 October 1915 in the First World War.

Pack Horse*, 8 Calder Street, closed in 1954

This house closed its doors many years ago and remained empty for some time, though the building still remains. Eventually it was taken over as offices by a firm of architects. It has also been a meeting place for the Church of Christ Scientist, who took the place in 1976. It is happily open once more for the selling of ale and is now the Concert Artists' Club. The old inn served as such, 'with tea rooms', until 1954. The frontage of the inn was rebuilt in 1895, to the design of Thomas Bell. The pub itself dates from around 1879, when Ellen Jackson was running the place, though in 1888, the owners were the Exors of Ann Roper. The Pack Horse was a Massey house. The name is fitting, for close by is the Salt Ford, (Salford) where the trains of pack horses carrying salt and other merchandise would cross the rivers Brun and Calder. The inn is reputed to be on the site a former farm.

Park View Inn*, Higgin Street

The Park View Inn dates from the 1870s, although rebuilt in 1905 when the place was advertised for sale in the *Burnley Gazette*, 25 April 1874. 'For sale,' the advert stated, 'the beerhouse known as the Park View Inn situated on Annie Street, Brunshaw Road, now in the occupancy of George Marchbank as tenant thereof'. The inn has been rebuilt since that date and more recently, extensive alterations and additions have been made. It is obvious which is the older part of today's building – that which bears the date, 1905 (see datestone on car park entrance side). It was built to a design of Angelo Waddington, whose initials can still be seen on the building. For many years, the landlord at the inn was Harry Reynolds, a cricket professional to the Turf Moor club during the late 1870s and early 1880s. Following Harry's death in 1894, his wife and son Billy took over the license and many humorous tales are told of Mrs Reynolds' minor clashes with her son during hours of opening. The name Park View is taken from the house name of James Nicholas Grimshaw of the Grimshaw Brewery Ltd at No. 157 Todmorden Road, Burnley. More modern extensions are on the front elevation of the pub and named 'the Lounge'.

Parker's Arms, 10/12 Croft Street, closed in 1958

Not to be confused with the old name for the Talbot and dating from the early 1860s, this house was converted from a number of cottages on Croft Street. The pub is still in living memory and was located near Peter Street on the old Pickup Croft – an area now taken by the bus station. The pub is mentioned in the *Burnley Advertiser*, 29 December 1877:

> The increase in value in public house property. On Thursday night, a large and respectable company assembled at the Parker's Arms when John Rawcliffe offered for competition that house. The bidding started with £2,500 by Mr Stanworth of the Cliviger Brewery and was run

The present Park View Inn dates from 1905, a date which can be seen on the car park side of the building.

up to £4,200 by Fernandez and Co. brewers. The premises were ultimately knocked down to Mr Grimshaw (Keirby Brewery Co.) for the handsome sum of £4,400. The auctioneer who formerly lived at the house stated after the sale, the late Mr Fletcher offered him the premises for '£1,400, which shows in an unmistakeable manner the extraordinary increase in value that has taken place during the last few years in connection with property of this character'.

Pedestrian Inn*, 30 Parker Lane, closed in 1933

This inn dated from around 1870 and was on, or very near, the site of the present Burnley Central Library. The cellar of the pub was reputed to be haunted and when the pub was demolished, the spirit was said to have transferred itself to the basement of the new library, now used as the reference department. Might this be the spectre of landlord Stephen Smith, who came to a violent end in 1879? Stephen was hit unprovoked by a former regular at the Pedestrian at the doorstep of the St Ledger across the road and subsequently died from his injuries. His assailant was later charged with manslaughter. For a brief period around 1923, the inn was tenanted by Tommy Boyle, the captain of Burnley FC's great triumphs all those years ago. The pub was obviously named after the method of travel on foot and would have been far more fitting in today's modern pedestrian complex.

Peel's Arms*, 109 Padiham Road, closed in 1978

This modest little pub enjoyed a lively existence until being demolished for the M65 motorway. The place started off as a beerhouse, which in 1871 was being run by Matthew and Martha Hartley, although the *Burnley Gazette* of 9 January 1875 tells us that the license was transferred from James Pooter to George Pooter. There was an incident concerning Pooter later that year, recorded in the *Burnley Gazette*, 25 December 1875:

> Bivell George Pooter, who keeps the Peel's Arms beerhouse, Westgate [?] was summoned for having his house open at 4.45 p.m. on Sunday the 12th inst., and Joseph Cowgill was summoned for aiding and abetting. PC Mitchell was going past the house and he saw Cowgill going away from the house. He followed him and found that he had half a gallon of beer under his coat, apparently fresh drawn. He took Cowgill back to the house and the landlord said the beer was filled before two o'clock. Fined 20s and costs and 5s and costs respectively, license not to be endorsed.

Many of the old regulars will recall Paddy McGinty, who used to run the New Hotel down Cog Lane as landlord of the Peel's. Tales might be told of the day a sign went up at the inn, put up by Paddy, saying 'no dogs allowed'. One particular regular brought into the pub a donkey insisting that the sign mentioned nothing of donkeys, and the beast defied all attempts to remove it. Common sense prevailed however when the animal decided to pass wind, and use the lobby of the pub as a toilet. The animal was soon ushered out of the pub then. Only Paddy McGinty could make the excuse that he was going for some change to his wife Lily and take a bag of coins to the Roebuck just up the road and come back blind drunk an hour or two later, forgetting where he had placed the bag of coins.

Plane Tree Hotel, Westgate

The original Plane Tree was built and occupied as a dwelling by Mr William Hopwood, alias 'Old Hopwood', a builder, mill owner and one of the richest men in town. Hopwood, or his descendants, were also responsible for the erection of much of the property in the Westgate area, including Oak Mount Terrace. Just before Christmas in 1915, Reginald Haslam left the Plane Tree Hotel, partially intoxicated and surrendered himself at police headquarters for the murder of his mistress, a crime for which he was later hanged. It is easy to see from the side elevation of the pub that the frontage has been added at some later date. This was the work of Burnley architect Charles Parsons, who designed the mock-Jacobean frontage of the Plane Tree which we see today in 1895-7. Some years later, the Plane Tree underwent extensive renovation and won an award from the Burnley Civic Trust. The building again recently stands empty.

Plane Tree*, Habergham, closed in 1937

The Plane Tree, a beerhouse in Habergham, was named after the plane tree, a local landmark that was situated about three hundred yards away from the junction with Rossendale Road and Cog Lane. The inn was behind what used to be the New Albion. The Plane Tree is clearly marked on the map of 1844. With the upgrading of Rossendale Road in the mid and late 1920s, the Plane Tree Inn was very much left in isolation being some distance away from the 'new' road.

The old Plane Tree at Habergham in its rural setting – notice the horse trough. (Towneley Art Gallery and Museums)

Probably the last tenant was Mary Wilkinson, who is listed in a directory for 1937. In September 1892 there was a brawl between two colliers at the inn, following which, one of them died from the injuries caused in the fight.

Poet's Corner, Curzon Street

This beerhouse was 'at the corner of Curzon Street, where Mrs Bracewell's dressmaking establishment was'. The pub here boasted a rat pit where, on one occasion, onlookers saw a dog kill 100 rats in 8 minutes – rat pits were a popular pastime at one time, with large wagers on the outcome. Mr Mosedale ran the inn or beerhouse, and it was he who took the lead in collecting signatures and forwarding petitions to the magistrates asking that theatrical licenses should be withdrawn. His need to collect the signature was probably boosted more by the fact that while people were in the theatres, they were not in pubs or beerhouses. Many people with strict religious views believed at this time that even a single visit to a theatre would jeopardise their hopes of heaven.

The following report was printed in the *Burnley Advertiser*, 2 March 1867:

> Breach of the Beer Act. Duke Wilkinson of the Poet's Corner beerhouse was summoned for having a disorderly house. PC Blackburn stated that he was on duty in Curzon Street on the night of the 11th inst. Hearing a great noise in the defendant's house, he went in. The defendant was stripped and fighting, and the house was in a very disorderly state. He told the defendant he should report him and he pulled out a shilling's worth of copper out of his pocket and offered it to him. Witness would not take it. Defendant then put it towards his coat and it fell on the floor. Defendant then sent a woman with 6d to treat him. Defendant said that the disorder of the house was nothing to do with him. There were some runners in from Glen View, where they had been running.

A person named Schofield came in and commenced to quarrel and fight with him, and he got well 'punched'. The police officer said that the man he was fighting with told him that the defendant was at fault, and he had hit him on the head with a stool. The defendant called a man named Benjamin Chaffer, who said he came from Blackpool. He was in the house at the time when Schofield came in and kicked up a quarrel with the runners. Defendant then sent a woman out for a policeman – a policeman came directly. The defendant had no chance of fighting, for he was being kicked. Did not hear one of the men say the defendant had struck him with a stool. Fined £5 and costs.

Prince Albert Inn, 91 Curzon Street, closed in 1987

The inn was named after Prince Consort and husband of Queen Victoria (1819-1861), which might give some indication of when the pub was built. This is just one of many pubs in Burnley with 'royal' connections. The Prince Albert was a homely little pub – albeit with some rather 'shady' customers in later years, until it succumbed to the demolition hammer in 1987.

Prince of Wales*, 79 Sandygate, closed in 1967

This little pub was situated between Ince Street and Lord Street on the old part of Sandygate. The inn dated from at least 1879 when Jimmy Heyes was running it. Jimmy was born in Haslingden, as was his wife, Isabella. Billy McFetridge, a popular footballer with the Burnley club, kept the pub in the 1890s. The title of the Prince of Wales is always conveyed to the eldest son of the reigning monarch of the United Kingdom.

Princess Alexandra, 78 Colne Road, closed in 1938

This public house dates from around the mid-1860s when Hezekiah Mitchell is listed as landlord. He later moved to the Barracks Tavern on Padiham Road. The name of the pub is taken from the consort of King Edward VII (1841-1910) and son of Queen Victoria. In later years, it became known simply as the Alexandra, and soon after closure became a block of flats. It was Mr Mitchell who introduced the varied displays of stuffed animals and a selection of 'rare walking sticks' that soon gave the name of 'Museum' to the inn. When Mr Mitchell removed to the Barracks Tavern on Padiham Road, he took with him his collection, and the name 'Museum' was transferred to the Barracks, a name used for the inn right up to its closure.

Princess Royal Hotel, 45/47 Yorkshire Street

Open at the time of writing, it has been known as the Clog and Spindle in more recent years, but happily, has reverted to its old name. In 1857, a notice appeared in the *Burnley Advertiser* in which Mr Thomas Sutcliffe 'begs to inform friends and the public that he has moved to the Princess Royal, Eastgate (now Yorkshire Street), opposite the lime kilns'. He further offered the services of post horses and carriages let out on hire, with a horse and cart available for removals. Alexander Bell, of the Clough Springs Brewery at Barrowford, owned the Princess Royal in the 1880s; the landlord and landlady at this time were James and Margaret Stuttard.

The 'Prinny', as it is called by locals, has recently undergone extensive alterations and, more importantly, gone back to its old name from the silly and obscure, 'Clog and Spindle'.

Queen's Hotel, 82 Curzon Street, closed in 1994

The Queen's Hotel was almost under the railway bridge on Curzon Street, though it was demolished in 1994, to make way for the supermarket. The inn was obviously named after Queen Victoria and her companion, Prince Albert was recalled in another pub just down the road until that too, was demolished. James Hartley ran the inn when it was called the Queen Victoria in 1854. It had become simply 'the Queen's' by 1868, although James was still mine host. The pub and its customers, in those far off days, would have looked out of the inn window to gaze upon the headgear workings of the old Parsonage Colliery directly across the way. Indeed, the Salford Mill was not far away and boasted in 1850 that it could obtain all the coal required from a pit 'only two minutes away'. The longest-serving landlord though must surely have been Walter Wray, who was there from 1908 through to 1937. The writer can remember going to the Queen's jug and bottle bar as a youngster to get crisps and pop after the nearby toffee shop had closed for the night, when he lived on Princess Street close by.

Railway Hotel, Rosegrove

Rather than the Railway Hotel, this house has always been known locally as the 'Red House', on account of it being brick-built. In fact, people have been known to look in the telephone directory for the number of the 'Red House'. The public house dates from 1856, when the place was advertised for sale by auction as being 'all newly erected'. However, it may have been rebuilt since that time. In the year 1881, the aged widow Nancy Kenyon was running the place. The following advertisement was printed in the *Burnley Advertiser*, 14 June 1856:

The Queen's on Curzon Street looking towards the town centre from the bottom of Railway Street. (Briercliffe Society)

The Queen's had become the Queens Head just before it was demolished and had undergone extensive restoration. The site today is just part of a supermarket car park and the inn could have been retained with a little forward planning. (Briercliffe Society)

Sale of inn or public house, to be sold by auction by Messrs Denbigh and Son at the house of Christopher Tattersall, the Railway Hotel situated in Rosegrove near Burnley in the County of Lancashire on Friday the 20th day of June 1856 at seven o'clock in the evening, subject to conditions of sale to be then and there produced. All that newly erected and good accustomed inn or public house known by the sign or name of the 'Railway Hotel' situated in Rose Grove near Burnley aforesaid, with the stable, coach house, yard and other outbuildings and premises therein belonging and in the occupation of Christopher Tattersall, the owner. The premises are held for a term of 999 years, subject to a yearly ground rent of £3 15s and to a nominal fine payable to the Lord of the Manor of Ightenhill. The above property is close to Rose Grove station of the East Lancashire Railway, and is situated at the junction of the roads leading from Burnley to Padiham and Accrington. For further information apply to Mr Tattersall, the owner, or at the office of Messrs Bollard and Mitchell, Solicitors, Burnley.

Railway Tavern*, 62 Bridge Street, closed in 1924

The license for this beerhouse lapsed in 1924 and a total of £3,100 was paid in compensation to Mrs S.A. Acomb, the last landlady here. The Brun House Building now occupies the site of the Railway Tavern. The tavern was at the junction of Parker Street and Bridge Street. The inn was once kept by John and Mrs Keirby, who also kept a brewhouse there. James Grimshaw married one of the Keirby daughters, and thus evolved James Grimshaw's Brewery, or Grimshaw's Brewery. The Railway Tavern remained in Grimshaw hands till closure. The tavern is mentioned in the *Burnley Gazette*, 25 December 1875:

Michael Smith was summoned for being drunk at the Railway Tavern at 10.50 p.m. on the night of the 11th inst. Inspector Weir and PS Wilkinson said he was so drunk that he could not walk. Mr Hartley, who appeared for the defendant called a witness to prove that Smith was not drunk, but he strengthened the evidence of the policemen, and the defendant was fined 5s and costs or seven days. George Bolland, the landlord was then charged with permitting drunkenness. When Inspector Weir called the attention of the landlady to the drunken state of Smith, she said she was very sorry. Two witnesses for the defence said Smith had not drunk any ale or tasted any. The daughter saw Smith in the room, but neither Bolland nor his wife had been in the room. They were in the kitchen and could see into the room where Smith was. Fined 20s and costs, or fourteen days, license not to be endorsed.

Red House, Curzon Street

The Red House is beerhouse on Curzon Street, mentioned in a court case and going from the information given, it could well have been named the Red-Light House. The following excerpt is taken from the *Burnley Express*, 14 January 1882:

Serious charge against a publican. Thomas Slater, landlord of the Red House, Curzon Street, appeared to answer a summons charging him with allowing his house to be used as a brothel. PS Blackburn and another proved the case, and the Bench fined him 5s and costs.

The Railway pub at Rosegrove is a brick-built structure and known by the locals as the 'Red House' for that reason.

Reindeer Hotel, Railway Street closed in 1998

The Reindeer pub was obviously built to cater for rail travellers and dates from around 1868, when Alice Rumley was running the place, though it appears to have been rebuilt. It was a Massey house back in 1888 and rated at £75. At this time, the Reindeer had a publican's license, as opposed to being a beerhouse.

Rifle Volunteer's, 1 Smalley Street

Originally the 'Royal Volunteer's Inn' was a beerhouse dating from around 1868, possibly the beerhouse noted as being on Smalley Street at that time run by Anthony Ashworth, who was also running the place in 1879. It is possible that the pub was named after the Burnley Volunteers (17th Lancashire Rifles), whose band not only won the admiration of all, leading marches through Burnley Streets, but also gave concerts in the Mechanic's to appreciative audiences. It also carried off first prize at Belle Vue at Manchester. It seems to have become the Rifle Volunteer's around 1890, when Charles Loder was the landlord, and it is listed under that name.

This photo shows the Reindeer and its sister pub, the Adelphi. Notice the conical tower on the Reindeer which was struck by lightening many years ago. (Briercliffe Society)

George Henry Frankland was licensee of the Rifle Volunteer's for twenty-three years. However, he used to tell the regulars he'd been a 'volunteer for forty-three years' – twenty-three as the licensee and twenty as a volunteer. As the latter he was a great enthusiast.

Roebuck Inn*, 128 Padiham Road, closed in 1978

The inn was kept during its final years by Jack Brennan, a man of dry wit. The inn was on the corner of Roebuck Street and Padiham Road. One night as a 'punishment' in the late sixties for something or other the younger lads had done, Jack removed the fuse from the jukebox, telling the lads that it was broken. They soon figured out what had taken place; one of the lads having a fuse, while another had a screwdriver. Once the 'repair' had been made, they asked Jack to turn the jukebox up, which he half-heartedly did, repeating his former statement that it was broken. When he heard the jukebox blasting out, everyone was barred, but only until the following day. The jukebox room was in a back place away from the bar and it wasn't unusual for one lad to go in and order several pints while all those who were barred entered through the back door. Jack was blissfully ignorant of the goings-on for many years. Another lad was in the habit of making paper tanks out of cigarette packets which were placed on all available shelves and window sills. The landlord was almost at the point of pulling his hair out wondering where all these cardboard

The Rifle Volunteer's has recently been extensively renovated following a fire at the place and is now open once again for trade.

tanks were coming from. The same lad 'discovered' the then new marker pens and their ability to draw on almost any surface, and promptly started drawing snoopy-type dogs all over the walls and windows, or anywhere else. This too, incensed Jack and one night he asked the waiter who was drawing snoopy dogs all over the pub. The waiter replied that he didn't know. 'You don't know,' replied Jack, 'tha's getten one painted on top of thi' bald head'.

Rose and Crown*, Manchester Road

The pub name has links with the Tudor Rose and the Crown of England. The inn dates at least from 1879, when a Thomas Rigby was running the place. It was a beerhouse at this time and has been rebuilt since around 1914, when a full license was passed from the closed Neptune Inn on Sandygate after a good deal of local opposition.

Rose and Thistle Hotel, 13 Grimshaw Street, closed in 1960

The Rose and Thistle was at the other end of the block that contains the Cattle Market Pub; the space it occupied is now being used as a small car park. David and Ellen Brown were running the Rose and Thistle in 1871, with their three children, Lucy, Martha and Sagar.

The old Rose and Crown, before being rebuilt. The present-day Rose and Crown dates from around the First World War. (Towneley Art Gallery and Museum)

Royal Butterfly Hotel, 83 Hufling Lane

As most people know, this hotel is named after a prize bull that belonged to the Towneleys. The inn was often frequented by the miners from Towneley Colliery, who often sat down on their haunches outside the pub on summer days, leaving a shiny mark on the wall. The pub has been extended in recent years and is now quite spacious compared to the 'old' Butterfly. I'm reminded of a customer in a pub looking for the telephone number of the Butterfly and being unable to find it looking under the 'Bs' when he should have been looking under 'Rs' for Royal Butterfly. But then the pub is known locally as the Butterfly. This is a common mistake when beer's in, and wits are out. The pub dates from the early 1870s when Thomas Lewis Barrett was landlord.

Royal Hotel, 27 Colne Road

An unpretentious little pub, the Royal Hotel was situated near the Colne Road library and across from the Wheatsheaf. In 1888, the pub was in private hands, belonging to the Exors of W. Brown, the pub was however tied to Grimshaw's ales, though later it was acquired by Massey's, following their take-over of Grimshaw's in 1928. A popular landlord at the Royal was 'Willie' Place, who was born at the Plane Tree Hotel, and thus instituted into the licensing trade at an early age. In his younger days, it was stated that there was no better all-round sportsman than Mr Place.

He played cricket and football and was a well-known wrestler. He was also an excellent roller-skater and more than handy with a billiard cue. One of his more unusual achievements was to jump over a fish cart in Bolton for a wager. When he died in 1948, he'd completed no less than sixty years in the pub trade. I think the pub closed down around the early 1970s.

Royal Oak Hotel, 107 St James's Street, closed in 1931

The Royal Oak Hotel was on the site of today's Marks & Spencer store and its license lapsed in 1931. The inn dated from around 1824, when William Maden was listed as the landlord here. He stayed until around 1834. The premises were originally a private dwelling. Sir Edwin Lutyens (1869-1944), an English architect on a visit to the town, referred to it as 'the best-designed building in Burnley'. Records tell us that the house was built on land known as Grimshaw's Croft. For a brief period around 1832, it was brought into use as the town's lock-up, and it also served as a courthouse during troubled times. In the early 1860s, the Royal Oak was under the command of Abraham Riley, but by 1888, the place was owned by James Folds, and a Grimshaw's House. The Royal Oak was also one of the sites in town from which Ned Robinson, the local bellman, paused to make his proclamations. The Royal Oak is mentioned in the *Burnley Advertiser*, 30 August 1856:

> Thomas Banister was charged with a serious assault on Hugh Sagar on Friday night near the Royal Oak tap. He had knocked Sagar down and kicked him on the neck. Fined £3 including costs, or, in default, two months.

On 3 October 1863, the same publication reported that:

> John Scanlon was charged by PC Beardsworth of being drunk and riotous on the night of Saturday the 19th inst. He was creating a disturbance near the Royal Oak tap. There were forty or fifty young men about and there appeared to have been a fight. When he got to the defendant, he commenced squaring and stripping himself to fight. He had to be taken away by force. It was half past eleven o'clock. Fined 5s and costs, in default seven days' imprisonment.

Another article concerning the pub was printed in the *Burnley Gazette*, 19 October 1872:

> Alice Chadwick, of the Royal Oak Inn, was summoned at the instance of PS Dillon for allowing prostitutes on her premises. The officer said that on Monday, the 7th inst., he heard a noise, and when they went in, two young men were scuffling on the floor. The manager said, 'you must be quiet now, they are here, I told you they were coming'. There were two reputed prostitutes in the lobby drinking with a man. A convicted thief was drunk. He returned again twenty minutes afterwards, and the prostitutes and thieves were all there. By Mr Baldwin: 'There were nine or ten people in the vault. A woman came in with a jug of beer, he left her there. I do not know who the woman was. Drink is served through a window in the lobby; this is separate from the vault. I went in by the Curzon Street door. PC Bland said he was in the company of PS Dillon on the night in question at half past nine. In his presence told the defendant she was harbouring thieves and prostitutes'. By Mr Baldwin: 'The prostitutes were quiet'. Mr Baldwin submitted that there was no case made out to render the defendant liable to the very severe penalty provided by the new Act. He was told that the women had been out, and returned again just before the policemen came…

Left: The Royal Oak stood on the corner of Curzon Street and St James's Street. (Briercliffe Society)

Opposite: The old Salford Hotel is now the Town Mouse public house.

Salford Hotel, 2 Royle Road, open at time of writing as 'Town Mouse'

A house once tottering on the brink of extinction was the Salford Hotel, adjoining Salford Bridge, where the Brun joins the Calder. Where the Salford pub is now, were private houses and a workshop in 1851. The original Salford house dates from around the mid-1860s, when Mary Tattersall was running the place. In 1871, it was Lucy Owen. A decade later, the pub landlord was Miles Wilkinson, who, along with his wife Mary and daughter Margaret, classed themselves as 'innkeepers'. The inn takes its name from the 'Salt Ford', at the point where the pack-horse trains crossed the rivers Calder and Brun. Indeed, the former Pack Horse pub lies just over the river from here to this day.

Frank Beattie Thomlinson, the stepson of the landlord, Mr Edward Nuttall, was awarded the Military Cross in 1916. On one occasion, Second Lieutenant Thomlinson went to the assistance of a wounded soldier, bandaging his wounds whilst in the shell-hole. He lifted him onto his back, and while going through the wire, a bullet from a sniper went through the wounded soldier's head and killed him instantly. In the 1920s, the Salford was tenanted by a member of Burnley FC's 1920/21 league championship squad, full-back Cliff Jones. The Salford closed around 1971, and remained so for about eight years before reopening as the 'Town Mouse'.

Scarlett Arms, 48 Howe Street, closed in 1913

This beerhouse was on Howe Street, a road which used to run almost parallel to St James's Street, from Hammerton Street to Manchester Road. It is now roughly the line of 'The Mall'. The Scarlett Arms was, of course, named after our famed general and one might wonder whether the old gentleman felt any pride at the house bearing his name, for it had neither architectural merit nor an agreeable interior. The premises, at a later date, became the Concert Artistes' Club and remained under that title until the whole block was demolished in the 1930s. The club then took over the former YMCA premises in St James' Row. The Scarlett dated from the early 1860s, when James Hile, who was born in Kettlewell, was running the place with his wife Ann, and their three children James, Sarah and John. The inn was also run by Henry Sharp, who is mentioned in court cases in April and May 1880. The *Burnley Advertiser* reported on 1 May 1880 that:

John Farmer was summoned for being drunk and Henry Sharp for permitting drunkenness. PC Neary said that the defendant was a licensed victualler and kept the Scarlett Arms Inn, in Howe Street, Burnley. About 10.30 on Saturday night, the 19th inst., he, in company with PC Smith visited the landlord's house, and saw in the back room three men, one of whom was the defendant. On the table there were four glasses, two of them half full of what appeared to be ale, and the contents of the others appeared to be spirits. The defendant Farmer was asleep at the time, and when he was awake, witness observed that he was drunk and said so. The defendant was afterwards ordered out of the house by the landlord and, on going out, he appeared to be falling, and would have done had it not been for a woman who prevented him. Several prostitutes were in the house. The defendant Farmer, when he entered the witness box denied that he was drunk, and said that he only had two quibs of beer. William Taylor was in the habit of waiting on at the defendant's house, and supplied the defendant Farmer with the drink. Henry Sharp, the landlord said that he had kept a public house about ten years, during which time he had only been fined twice. The defendant Sharp was fined 10s and costs, and the defendant Farmer, 5s and costs.

The last landlord at the Scarlett Arms would appear to have been Thomas Bullock in 1911 and its license lapsed in 1913, when a total of £3,250 was paid out in compensation.

Shepherd's Arms, 69-71 Cog Lane

Originally a beerhouse named the Peeping Tom in 1878, the address of the pub is recorded as No. 71 Cog Lane, and remained as such until 1887. The landlord at this time was John Magnall with his wife, Sarah, who held a remarkable record serving ale at the pub. John Magnall, however, was not a local lad; he was born in Tottington around 1847. The name, 'Peeping Tom' has no obvious local connection; Peeping Tom is, of course, the Coventry tailor said to have peeped at Lady Godiva. Shortly after 1887, the inn is renamed the 'Shepherd's' though to this day it's still referred to by nearly all the locals as the 'Peeps', but probably few know that it is in fact an abbreviation of the original name. John Magnall continued running the inn right up to 1902, but the family connection doesn't stop there; Sarah Magnall, John's widow, was the landlady right up to 1914.

Ship Inn, 34 Finsley Gate, closed in 1936

The license for this public house lapsed in 1936, when a total of £2,235 was paid in compensation. An early landlord here was Richard Pratt, who also owned Pratt Row near Reedley on the road from Lane Head to Brierfield. William Pickering kept the Ship during its later years, though Ethel Sutcliffe was the last landlady there. The Ship Inn was roughly where the tyre depot is today, near the junction of Finsley Gate and Parker Lane. The *Burnley Advertiser* records one instance when the landlord was summoned to court, 11 January 1868:

> Selling a little on the sly. Thomas Whitaker, landlord of the Ship Inn, Lane Bridge (the old name for Finsley Gate) was summoned for a breach of the Licensing Act on the 25th inst. PS Slatters said that at thirty-five minutes past three o'clock in the afternoon of Christmas Day, he visited the house of the defendant and found the front door open, and the room full of company, some of whom were drunk. The policeman asked him how long it was, to which he replied that he had been 'doing a bit on the sly'. The Bench fined him £3, including costs.

Sportsman's Arms Foundry Street (Finsley Gate)

Another beerhouse of which little is known, apart from that below. Foundry Street was the old name for that end of Finsley Gate nearest to Manchester Road. Reference to the pub is made in the *Burnley Advertiser*, 24 October 1863:

Robert Brunton of the Sportsman's Arms, Foundry Street was charged with having his house open during illegal hours. PC Lord said that on Sunday morning the 11th inst., he visited the house of the defendant. It was about thirty-five minutes past eight o'clock. He found three men in each with a glass of ale before them. The men lived in the neighbourhood. Fined 10s and costs.

Spread Eagle, 15 Temple Street, closed in 1969

An inn dating from around the 1860s, John Hartley was landlord here in 1868. In 1871, David Dyson Smalley, who is described as a 'master joiner', ran the inn along with his wife Margaret. The couple were still there a decade later. A family with a long acquaintance with the inn were the Cudsworths: first George Henry from 1892 to 1908, and then Henry and Abraham until 1914. The site of the Spread Eagle has now been taken by the Higher Tentre Housing Scheme.

St Leger Hotel, 15/17 Red Lion Street, closed in 1957

St Leger and a number of other town inns were sacrificed in 1963, along with Pickup Croft, to make way for the bus station and adjacent approaches. Matthew and Mary Stuttard were running the St Leger in 1871, when it was simply referred to as being a beerhouse. The hotel is mentioned in the *Burnley Advertiser*, 22 October 1864:

> Assault. Mary Stuttard, whose husband keeps a beerhouse in Red Lion Street, was summoned for an assault on Eliza Medley on Monday week. The complainant went into the house to seek her husband and, on finding him there, said she had rather found him somewhere else. Defendant said her words were, 'she had rather he had been in Wapping' and this was confirmed by a witness on behalf of the defendant. Some other provocative language passed, and the assault complained of took place, which was confirmed by a witness called by the complainant. The Bench considered there had been a great provocation given and dismissed the case.

The pub is mentioned a second time in the *Burnley Gazette*, 10 May 1873:

> John Marshall, a chimney sweep residing in Cannon Street, Burnley was summoned for allowing a boy underage to descend a chimney. PS Rainey saw the boy cross Manchester Road, and followed him to the St Leger Inn. When the sergeant got there, the boy was in the chimney and he saw the boy come down. The defendant admitted to him that he had been cautioned. The boy was sixteen years of age, and the Act prohibits under twenty-one. Fined 2s 6d and costs.

Stanley Arms, 164 Oxford Road

The Stanley dates from about 1870; the following year, James and Margaret Yates were running the inn. The pub sign bears the arms of the Earls of Derby who were the Stanley family from 1485.

Star Inn, 2 Hill Top Street, closed in 1919

The Star's license lapsed in 1919, when a sum of £5,020 was paid in compensation. A larger sum than that was paid out for the closure of beerhouses. Hill Top Street was where the first Sainsbury's store was, near the Keirby roundabout: the house was originally the mill manager's house at Rishton Mill and built by the mill's owners, the Folds. As an inn, it dated from about 1834, when John Taylor was running it, and in the early 1860s, the place was also home to landlord Henry Ratcliffe and his wife, Alice who were both born Loveclough way. By the early 1870s through to 1879, George Sutcliffe was landlord here. Edward Thomas was probably the last landlord here – he is listed in 1914. Many may recall that the annual fair was held in this area for a short period of time. On 15 January 1859, the *Burnley Advertiser* reports that:

> William Proctor was summoned for an assault on Ellen Whittaker in the Star Inn tap on Monday 3rd inst. The complainant said that Proctor was in the tap. When she asked him for 25s that he owed her husband, he struck her in the face. Proctor denied that he had struck her. Fined 1s and costs.

The inn is mentioned again in the Burnley Advertiser, on 18 June 1863:

> Rueben Proctor was charged with striking PC Eccles at the door of the Star Inn tap on Saturday night. He had been fetched to the tap by Proctor's wife who said that a man had been striking her in there. At the door he met the defendant who was rather fresh in liquor, and whom he advised to go home. Upon which, he struck the constable on the nose causing it to bleed freely. Fined 10s and costs.

Stork Hotel, 102 Westgate, closed in 1989

The Stork dates from around 1868 when William Duckett was running the inn. By the early 1880s, the hotel was being run by the widow Sarah Duckett and her four children Charles, Thomas, Elizabeth and Ann – all 'assistant innkeepers'. The Stork is reputed to be haunted by the spectre of an old gentleman in a flat cap who tours the landing upstairs at night – he was seen regularly by some of the last landlords before the inn closed down altogether in 1989. Today, the Stork Hotel on Westgate still survives but it has been converted into an insurance office.

Sun Inn, 4a Bridge Street, closed in 1925

This inn was on Bridge Street in the town centre and closed in 1925, the premises being converted into Hudson's leather shop. A total of £4,750 was paid out for this inn, the high cost reflecting its close proximity to the town centre. The inn, at one time, was the home of Miles Veevers, who was also the constable of the town, and it was also the meeting place of the churchwardens who gave out relief to the poor. A stone over the doorway bore the date '1790'. Alice Veevers was famed for her cooked hams, which she hung from the ceiling of the inn, and was landlady here in 1824. Many travellers to the town stayed at the Sun Inn, preferring its more homely atmosphere to that of the Bull Hotel. February 1927 saw the death of James Parker, who had kept the inn for twenty years. He started work at the age of fourteen at the Keirby Brewery

Above: This Oxford Road pub is named after the Stanley family, who at one time were the richest landowning family in England.

Right: The only known photo of the Star Inn is this one taken through the Triumphal Arch on Church Street erected for the visit of Prince Albert who came to open the Victoria Hospital in 1886. (Towneley Art Gallery and Museum)

The Sun Inn on Bridge Street was famed for Dame Veever's hams, which hung from the roof beams at the old inn. (Briercliffe Society)

The old Swan Inn is still very much a feature of Burnley town centre.

where he worked for eighteen years. Mr Parker then took over the Sun Inn, retiring in 1912. James was never married, though his widowed sister, Mrs Schofield, acted as housekeeper for him. The inn is mentioned in the *Burnley Advertiser*, 14 January 1865:

> Martha Stowell, wife of William Stowell of the Sun Inn tap was charged with stealing nineteen sovereigns, and about sixteen shillings in silver, the property of John Thornber of Hellifield near Skipton, Yorkshire on Wednesday the 4th inst. The sovereigns were in a purse and the silver loose in the pocket of the prosecutor. It appeared that on the day named, the prosecutor was with the prisoner at the Mason's Arms tap. He fell asleep and the prisoner took the money from him in that state, and in the presence of the wife of the keeper of the tap, who remonstrated with her for taking it, and told her she did not allow such work there, there would be something done about it. When the prosecutor awoke, he felt his pockets and, finding his money gone, he asked about it of a man who was in the tap. He said he knew nothing at all about it and called for the landlady to come in. The prosecutor then asked her about the loss of his money and she told him she knew all about it, the Mrs at the Sun tap had taken it. They then went down to the Sun Inn tap, and the prosecutor asked the prisoner for his money. On her refusing to give it him…Committed for trial at the next sessions, bail was accepted.

The old cells still survive behind the Swan Inn and are now used as the men's toilets.

Swan Hotel, 44 St James's Street

Swan Inn, which retains its 'olde worlde' charm, is very much a long-standing feature of Burnley town centre. Mr David Homer, a prominent local tradesman of the past, said: 'the Swan was regarded as a famous posting house for coaches between Manchester and Skipton and had the honour of entertaining nightly the worthy tradespeople of Burnley who would drop in for a market glass on Mondays and a night-cap on other evenings and discuss the latest news and prices'. In the mid-1800s, the genial and popular landlord was Christopher ('Kit') Edmondson. He held the license for forty years and was well respected and kept an orderly house. Kit also farmed land in nearby Pickup's Croft and kept a butcher's shop next door to the pub. The Swan was offered for sale on 28 August 1851 by auction at the Swan itself, and was described as:

> Lot 8: All that messuage inn or public house called the Swan Inn with the brewhouse, stable, taproom, yards and premises thereto (being corner premises) fronting on the Old Market Place, in Burnley and adjoining lots 13 and 14 and the court and passage from the Market Place to Red Lion Street aforesaid. Tenant, Thomas Diggle, innkeeper.

At the turn of the nineteenth century, the town's lock-up was in Fleet Street – a short street swallowed up by the new shopping precinct in the early 1960s. In 1819 it was decided to make use of land in Red Lion Street to build a new jail, which was erected at the rear of the Red Lion Hotel and the Swan Inn. The building soon acquired the name of the 'black 'oyle'.

In later years, the prison transferred to Keighley Green police headquarters. On 21 February 1856, the *Burnley Advertiser* reports a robbery at the Swan Inn:

On Sunday evening between seven and eight o'clock, a young man, a stranger, somewhat shabbily-dressed in dark velveteen jacket, and plain light fustian trousers went into the house of Mr Thomas Diggle, the Swan Inn, St James's Street, and asked for lodgings for the night. He said he had relatives in the town, but had not been able to make them out. He was shown into the front parlour, where he sat down among the company. While there, he ate something which he took from his pocket, and on being asked to drink by those present he declined, saying he had not taken anything of the sort for some time. About a quarter past eleven o'clock, he was shown to a bed in the topmost room of the house, in which were several beds, one of which was occupied by an ostler. No candles were left with him, and the light came from the obelisk in the middle of the street, shining into the room and rendering one unnecessary. Mr Diggle retired to rest about twelve o'clock. It appears that sometime early on Monday morning the stranger took from the box belonging to the ostler, which was in the bedroom and unlocked a pair of new stockings, a silk handkerchief, a waistcoat, and a pair of trousers. Descending into a lower room, where some of the family slept, he took from the trouser pocket of Mr Diggle's oldest son (who is in business as a grocer), his shop door key, and the key of his safe. He then went down by some means, there being no sign of force, opened the lock of a drawer in the bar, and took about 30s and a bottle belonging to another son, and several other articles of dress. The keys taken from the pocket of the eldest son were found on the stand of the bar; he also left the ostler's trousers on a chair in the back kitchen. He left the house by the door of this kitchen which opens into the back of the premises, leaving it unclosed. The ostler got up about five o'clock in the morning and, finding the kitchen door opened, and other signs of what had taken place, immediately awoke Mr Diggle. It was found that the thief had never been in bed and no clue has yet been found.

In the early 1860s, the Swan was ably run by Mary Diggle with the assistance of Jane, her daughter, and a decade later by Edward Diggle and his sister Jane. Some years ago, the Swan was reputed to be possessed by spirits other than those served behind the bar and the landlord and his family were often plagued by the mysterious antics of a 'presence' who unaccountably removed household articles from customary places, even behind locked doors. Happily, the matter was seemingly resolved and the 'visitations' ceased... or have they?

Tackler's Arms, 13 Temple Street, closed in 1910

This beerhouse was formerly known as the Boar's Head; the license for this pub lapsed in 1910, when £2,500 was paid out in compensation. The inn was on the corner of Ashworth and Temple Street, next to the Spread Eagle. By 1923, the building had been turned into the Dawson's shop, but by 1945 it had become the home of J. Naughton, a labourer. The last landlord here was Harold Reynolds.

Talbot Hotel, 2 Talbot Lane, (the old address)

Originally known as the Parkers' Arms, so named on account of its association with the Towneley-Parkers of Royle, this pub formerly stood at the corner of Shorey Street, behind a block of old cottages. At its rear, there was a brewhouse, stables and garden and we are told, 'there

were quaint oak panelling and nooky stairs inside; while outside was the well-known riding block'. The Talbot of today bears two datestones: '1626' (on the side of the building) and '1888' (on the front of the building). The present building dates from the latter date. Grace Ingham kept the tavern in 1747 and provided food for those engaged in repairing the church tower of St Peter's at that time. Thomas Crossley, who used to have the Talbot, also had a small croft near the canal bridge up Colne Road and a field of about seven acres where clay was dug for making bricks. The barn doors of the old Talbot were also utilised for the posting and displaying of town notices. The pub is mentioned in the *Burnley Advertiser*, 7 February 1857:

Return of a Crimean soldier. On Monday evening week, the bells of St Peter's rang out a merry peal to welcome the return of Mr James Howarth, son of Mr John Howarth, Church Street. Mr Howarth is in the Royal Artillery and was about twelve months before Sebastopol. On Saturday evening last, about fifty of the friends and relations of the young soldier met to celebrate his return at the house of Richard Boys, the Talbot Inn. About six o'clock they sat down to dinner, the tables being amply furnished with most excellent fare, served up in the best style. After dinner, Mr D. Harrison was called to preside. At the call of his friends, Mr Howarth entered into his experience during the great siege, giving details of 'moving accidents' and 'hair-breadth escapes' in the imminent deadly breach. During the evening, 'the Queen', 'the army and the navy' and other toasts were given and drunk with cheers. The health of the returning soldier was received most enthusiastically, and suitably responded to.

Right: The Thorn Hotel, still sadly missed by many, was for many years the home of George Chester Ogden, whose name can be seen over the door here. (Briercliffe Society)

Opposite: The old Talbot Hotel before being rebuilt in 1888. (Briercliffe Society)

Thorn Hotel, 67 St James's Street, closed in 1965

Almost directly across from the Bull was the Thorn Hotel, again a former farm. One of the first records of this place is from 1545, when Robert Mitchell rented and occupied a farm known as 'the Thorn' from the landlord, Lawrence Towneley. The Thorn, in 1792, was kept by William Beanland, who, in 1824, described himself as 'a gentleman', though he was now living at Paradise Row. We know that John Wesley (1703-1791) preached from a mounting stone at the Thorn at the age of eighty-three years. However his hostile sermon angered the Burnley crowd, who then chased the old gentleman down nearby Wapping. Luckily, he escaped by hiding in an outside 'privy' and was saved from any violent attack by the angry mob. In more placid times, George Chester Ogden was landlord at the Thorn Hotel for twenty-nine years from August 1873 to 1902 – he died in September 1909. George was the son of Thomas Ogden who, at one time, kept the White Horse Hotel on St James's Street. George Chester was born in Manchester around 1854, and his wife, Annie Elizabeth was a Chorley girl by birth. Annie Elizabeth died at their Ormerod Street home in November 1901. George Chester was a keen swimmer in his younger days, and was the winner of a swimming race on the canal from the canal bridge at Ormerod Road to Manchester Road Bridge. George C. Ogden died in September 1909 at his home, No. 71 Ormerod Road, following a prolonged illness. Of all the buildings that disappeared during the 1960s, the Thorn was missed the most. The Thorn is mentioned in the *Burnley Gazette*, 25 May 1872:

Felony at the Thorn Hotel. Joseph Jackson was charged with stealing from the Thorn Inn on Saturday last, four knives, four forks – the property of Squire Greenwood. The case was clearly made out and the prisoner was sentenced to imprisonment in the House of Correction for fourteen days.

Three Horse Shoes*, 22 Boot Street, closed in 1907

License for this beerhouse lapsed in 1907, when £1,000 was paid in compensation under the Licensing Act of 1904. It later became J. Murray's lodging house and if it existed today would be slap-bang in the middle of the bus station. The beerhouse appears to have dated from around the late 1860s, when it was an unnamed beerhouse, but at this address and run by Joseph Harling. The last landlord was probably T. Lock. On 15 February 1873, the *Burnley Gazette* reports that, 'the license held by James Toothill of the Three Horse Shoes beerhouse was transferred to James Gallagher'.

The pub is mentioned in connection with another event in the *Burnley Advertiser*, 1 May 1880:

Thomas Conroy, a militiaman, was charged with being drunk. PC Gallaghan stated that on Saturday night about half past ten he was called to the Three Horse Shoes inn to eject the prisoner who was drunk and riotous. On the way to the police station, the prisoner kicked him (witness) several times... Fined 10s and costs for the assault and 5s and costs for being drunk and riotous.

Tim Bobbin Inn, Padiham Road

This ancient inn is named after John Collier, alias Tim Bobbin. He was the son of John, a minister of the Established Church, and died 14 July 1876, aged seventy-eight years. He was buried at Rochdale churchyard along with his wife, Mary. Tim Bobbin's claim to fame is the many Lancashire dialect poems he composed, and the following epitaph written by him was placed on his tomb by his grandson in 1878:

Here lies John and with him Mary
Cheek by jowl, and never vary
No wonder they so well agree
John wants no punch and Moll no tea.

Quite why the pub is named after Tim Bobbin is something of a mystery, as there is no hard evidence that he ever visited Burnley, although it is known that he wrote to the Towneley family. The Tim Bobbin inn is of some antiquity, formerly a farm cottage dwelling in a then isolated district. It was rebuilt in 1701. One of the first references to the inn was in 1828 when the landlord was John Hargreaves. During the days of cockfighting, the Tim Bobbin was said to be the favourite place for this 'sport' in the locality. The inn was mentioned during agitations of 1842. Called by striking weavers, the Burnley men met outside the Tim Bobbin and resolved to march on to Blackburn. They set off on 15 August but were stopped by the police and made to

The old Tim Bobbin was formerly a farm belonging to the Shuttleworths of Gawthorpe Hall, near Padiham. (Briercliffe Society)

The Tim Bobbin public house we know today. (Briercliffe Society)

disband. They regrouped and attempted to stop the Habergham Eves coal pit, but the magistrates again called out the military; the Riot Act was read and the mob dispersed. Tales are told of how one man at the Tim Bobbin offered the sale of his wife in 1880 for half a crown, the offer was quickly taken up and money exchanged hands. The man who sold his wife, however, relented and bought her back.

One of the longest-serving landlords at Tim Bobbin must surely be James Kenyon, who was mine host for thirty-four years. James died in August 1907. Besides his position as landlord, he also served as a guardian and a representative of Ightenhill district on the Rural District Council. His son served his time as a veterinary surgeon, and went on to become the Borough Veterinary Inspector for the town. Frank Turner, the son of Fanny and the late Edward Ralph Turner of the Tim Bobbin, was killed in the First World War. Today the Tim Bobbin is a thriving traditional Lancashire pub, steeped in history.

Tradesmen's Arms*, 210 Accrington Road, closed in 1912

The Tradesmen's Arms was on the site of the Kwik Save store on Accrington Road, and was formerly named the Collier's Arms. The Collier's Arms, quite apt for this area of town with all its miners in the early 1880s, was run by James Sagar, with help from his wife, Elizabeth, as a 'beer and butcher's shop'. Its license lapsed in 1912, when a sum of £1,600 was paid in compensation for the beerhouse. It became the Tradesman's Arms around 1887, when Francis Stuttard was running the place.

Trafalgar Inn, 42 Trafalgar Street, closed in 1958

The Trafalgar Hotel (as it was known later) faced the canal footbridge on Trafalgar before being demolished to make way for the Trafalgar flats there in the 1960s. The inn was one of the few in town that served Dutton's ales. The inn dated from around 1854, when William Chadwick was running it. However, in a directory of 1868, it is not named, though the address is the same, and the place, at this time, was being run by James Smith. The pub is mentioned in the *Burnley Advertiser*, 12 September 1863:

> Breach of the Licensed Victualler Act. Samuel Hartley of the Trafalgar Inn was summoned for breach of this act. PC Lord said that he visited the house at twelve noon on Sunday the 30th inst. Previous to going in, he saw a woman come out of the tap. He followed her and heard her say, 'the police'. Some persons went upstairs, he followed and found a man and a woman – he knew the woman, she lived in town. In the bar there were some glasses, part-full of ale. The defendant said that he was sorry for what had happened, he had not kept the inn for long, and he would take more care in the future. Fined 10s and costs.

The pub was named after the Battle of Trafalgar. It's also interesting to note that the names of all the flats that took the place of the inn also had names connected with this battle. On 2 August 1918, Maurice James Renwick, aged twenty years and the son of Minnie Langley (formerly Renwick) and William Arthur Renwick was killed in the First World War – just one of many local victims of the conflict.

The Turf Hotel we see today has some rather ornate stonework, with arched windows and carvings around its doorway.

The Union Hotel can be seen here on the right of this photograph taken in 1974. Someone stated that the Union looked like a public toilet with all the tiles on the front elevation. (Briercliffe Society)

Turf Hotel, 49 Yorkshire Street

Formerly the Turf Inn, or even the Turf Tavern, this pub was originally a beerhouse, dating from around 1848, when William Gray was running the place. By the early 1880s the landlord and landlady were George Hitchon Cudworth and his wife Sarah. Benny Cross, a prominent member of Burnley League championship team of 1920/21, also had a spell as landlord at the hotel; he is listed in directories for 1937. The Turf is mentioned in the *Burnley Advertiser*, 18 December 1858:

> Robbery. Esther Stansfield and Agnes Featherstone were charged with stealing £2 10s in gold from the person of Abraham Berry on the afternoon of Tuesday last. It appears that Esther Stansfield keeps the tap belonging to the Turf Tavern. About two o'clock on the afternoon of Tuesday, the prosecutor went into the tap, which is under the tavern. When he went in he found only the two women named. He treated with two glasses of ale, and afterwards when he wished to leave, they took his hat and refused to let him have it, unless he paid for something more. He then paid for some rum, spending about two shillings in all. He then got up and expressed his determination to leave. The women stuck to his hat, but when they saw that he was going, they seized him and one of them put her hand in his pocket and took there from two sovereigns and a half. As soon as he could get liberty he left the tap and gave the information to the police. The tap-keeper was taken into custody, but no money was found upon her. Featherstone was found in the Turf Tavern later and she was taken into custody, no money was found on her. The prosecutor, who is an elderly man, positively swore to them having taken his money, so the magistrates committed them both for trial at the next Preston Sessions.

Union Hotel*, 145 Padiham Road, closed in 1978

The name of the inn has nothing to do with trade unionism; the pub is more than likely named after the Union Turnpike Trust Road that ran along side, or Padiham Road. One of the first references to the Union was when it was still a beerhouse in 1871, and David and Alice Shepherd were running it. The Union Hotel was kept for many years by John Willie Walsh, the well-known local wrestler. The Union Hotel finally closed its doors on Monday 27 November 1978. The last landlord and landlady were Colin and Kath Holmes.

Victoria Inn*, 86 Colne Road

The inn obviously takes its name from Queen Victoria and gives us some indication of when it was built, although originally the place was a beerhouse named the Cobblers Rest. The Halsteads – William and Samuel – kept the inn during the 1890s. The *Burnley Gazette*, 15 May 1875, announces when, 'the license from the Cobblers Rest was transferred from John Smith to Halstead Haworth'.

Waggoner's Inn, 168 Colne Road

The name of the inn reflects a slower mode of transport and the pub dates from around the 1870s. Wilfred Pollard, son of Mr and Mrs Pollard of the Waggoner's Inn, was killed on 8 October 1917 in the First World War.

This inn, formerly the Queen Victoria and a beerhouse named the Cobblers Rest are both still with us on Colne Road.

Water Street Tavern*, 27, 29 and 31 Water Street

Yet another of those taverns down the old Wapping part of Burnley. The Water Street Tavern is mentioned, though not by name, only by address, in 1868, when it was being run by Henry Whittaker. The *Burnley Gazette*, of 25 April 1874, advertised the inn for sale as follows: 'for sale, the beerhouse known as the Water Street Tavern situated in Water Street, Burnley in the occupation of David Jolly as tenant thereof'. The sale was evidently not taken up, for David Jolly is still listed as landlord of the beerhouse in 1879. Water Street ran off Cannon Street at right angles and up to St James's Street.

Waterloo Hotel, 39 Trafalgar Street

The landlord here in 1976/77 was Jack Duckworth, but not the character from Coronation Street! The building still exists and will be part of the future development of the Weaver's Triangle. It was at the Waterloo Hotel that forty-three-year old William Crossley went for a drink before viciously murdering Mary Ann Allen with an axe at her home in Lomas Street off Trafalgar on 11 June 1894. A more detailed account of this murder can be seen in Leslie Chapple's *East Lancashire Murders*.

The Wellington was often the first port of call for fans going to see the team at Turf Moor football ground. (Briercliffe Society)

Weaver's Arms*, 126 St James's Street, closed in 1909

This building, although no longer serving its original purpose, still stands just above the former model shop on St James's Street above the Cross Keys. Its license lapsed in 1909, when £1,600 was paid out in compensation for the beerhouse.

Well Hall Hotel, Church Street, closed in 1958

The hotel named the Well Hall was built in 1873 on the site of a building known as Well Hall belonging to Dr William Greenwood, who is listed as a 'gentleman' in a directory of 1824. When the Church Literary Institute opened on Manchester Road in 1850, the extensive library of the late Dr William Greenwood was donated to it forming the basis for a large collection of books here. Well Hall was formerly a farmhouse with outbuildings and a smithy here was thought to have been used for the manufacture of firearms, hence the name of the old thoroughfare that used to stand here, 'Gunsmith Lane'. The Well Hall is said to have had a well some 120ft deep later used by the Keirby Brewery. There was a particularly sad accident at the Well Hall Brewery in June 1855, which was reported in the *Burnley Advertiser*:

> A lamentable accident occurred at Well Hall Brewery, in Church Street, about three o'clock in the afternoon of Monday last. Mr John Keirby, the proprietor of the brewery, had just gone into the room containing the liquor boiler, which is in an upper storey, when he was followed by his only son, (also named John), a child about three years of age. Mr Keirby, as we understand, took the child in his arms, and at the moment he had done this, the boiler burst at its side, the child

was scalded to death almost instantly, and Mr Keirby himself severely injured by the steam and liquor from the boiler. The building containing the boiler rises at the back of the premises in Church Street, and is connected therein. The building itself does not appear to have sustained any injury. Other parties connected with the brewery were about at the time, but being below, fortunately escaped.

Wellington Arms, 2 Todmorden Road, has now changed its name to the Duck and Boot

This still-thriving public house dates from around the late 1860s, when Sarah Parker is listed as landlady with her three children on what was then Fulledge Road. She was still there in 1871 according to the census return. The Wellington was one of two in the town (you might say that we had a 'pair of Wellingtons') and this particular one changed its name to the Wellington Hotel and now, the Duck and Boot. They are both named after the Iron Duke, Arthur Wellesley (1769-1852). The Wellington Arms is mentioned in the *Burnley Gazette*, 1 February 1888:

> Daring Burglary in Burnley. Early yesterday morning the Wellington Arms, situated at the corner of Todmorden Road and Brunshaw Road was entered by thieves, and several pounds worth of clothing and spirits etc. were taken away. Mr John Crossley, the landlord, his family and servants retired about midnight on Monday and the neighbours state that they heard noises near the beerhouse an hour later. The thieves (for there are indisputable traces of there having been two of them) appear to have climbed over the six-foot-high wall on the Todmorden Road side and using some sharp instrument, forced the catch of the bar on the parlour window. These operations were carried out during the long continuing barking of the Skye terrier that has been kept at night in the kitchen on the opposite side of the lobby to the bar parlour. But the thieves coolly shut the dog up in the scullery when they got inside and prevented him making too much noise…

Another popular landlord was Alfred Heap, a member of a respected Fulledge family who also operated butcher's shop next door to the inn on Todmorden Road. Alfred was landlord at the Wellington from 1914 to his death in March 1922.

Wellington Inn, Robert's Row off Manchester Road

No one living will recall this inn, which was situated at No. 287 Manchester Road just lower down than the General William's; it became the Victoria Wine shop, and has been extensively altered in more recent years. The pub ran from around 1868, when Ann Almond was landlady, as reported in the *Burnley Advertiser*, 1 February 1868:

> Ann Almond who keeps the Wellington Inn, Robert's Row was summoned for breach of the Licensing Act. PC Bradshaw said that at five minutes past twelve o'clock on the morning of the 20th inst., the defendant's son brought half a gallon of ale out of the house and took it to a house across the way. He said he was taking it to a wedding party. Defendant said she was in bed at the time, and did not know about it. On account of the previous good character of the house, the Bench only inflicted a fine of 5s and costs.

Possibly, increased competition from the Rose and Crown and the General William's caused the closure of the old Wellington Inn, although the exact date of closure is unknown.

Wheatsheaf*, 29 Croft Street, closed in 1907

This house was located No. 29 Croft Street, a place later taken by Collinge's ironmongers and later still the site of the entrance to Kwik Save. In the early 1860s, the Wheatsheaf was being run by Richard Whitehead, 'beer-seller and grocer', with his wife, Sarah. In August 1902 the landlord here, William Eastwood, was in court for harbouring women of low character, and for permitting drunkenness. On 23 July that year the premises were watched for five and a half hours, during which time twenty-three visits were made by five women. One woman was seen to go in ten times, and another six times, one staying as long as fifty-five minutes. The Bench found the case proved and fined the landlord £10 and costs, though his license was not endorsed.

White Bull Inn, Gannow Lane, closed in 1978

White Bull Street survives off Gannow Lane to recall this Burnley pub, which in the 1880s was owned by Shaw and Co., a Blackburn brewery. It was later taken over by Thwaites' Brewery. The pub dated from around 1868, when William Whittaker was running it. The inn was on the right-hand side of Gannow Lane from Gannow Top, and was demolished during the construction of the Gannow Top Roundabout, and the making of the M65 motorway. On 10 May 1873, the *Burnley Gazette* reported that:

> Jane Birch was charged with stealing £39 in gold from the White Bull Inn, Habergham Eves kept by Thomas Maney. Maney said the prisoner had lodged at his house with a man whom she called her husband for about eleven months. On Monday the 25th of November last, she went to his house with another woman, and asked for each of them a glass of beer. She had left about a week before and had come to collect her clothes. The prisoner left about half past six on the night of the 25th inst. Between ten and eleven o'clock that night, he missed £39 in gold which was in a leather purse fastened around with a elastic band, inside a jug. The jug was placed in an opening down the cellar steps…

White Hart, (New White Hart) 45 Church Street

Properly, this pub is the New White Hart, the present building opening on 12 April 1956. The opening ceremony was performed by Ronnie Clayton, a former boxing champion. The pub boasted at the time of being the first post-war public house to be built in Burnley. First landlord at the new pub was Geoffrey Greenwood, a former steward at the Ighten Mount bowling club. The bar at the new pub was stated to be 28ft feet long, possibly the longest in Burnley? The tavern originally began in 1735 as a dwelling-house under the name of the Three Tuns. In 1811, without doubt to celebrate Lord Nelson's naval successes, it became the Lord Nelson Inn, but in 1838 it became the White Hart. With the widening of Church Street, the hotel was demolished and rebuilt further back in 1956, then renamed New White Hart. The inn was a Thwaites' house back in 1888, when it was rated at £68 10d. The sign of the White Hart is said to be one of

This photograph of the old White Hart gives the reader an idea of where the old pub was located and how prominent a building it was on Church Street. (Briercliffe Society)

the commonest in England; the sign of Richard II is a white hart with a collar of gold. James Fryer was another landlord at the White Hart from around 1914 – James was a manufacturer at Foulridge before coming to Burnley. He died in July 1926. His wife Annie Elizabeth kept the pub on after James' death until she retired to Marton. The pub is mentioned in the *Burnley Advertiser*, 1 May 1880:

> Disturbance at a public house. Robert Wilson, landlord of the White Hart Hotel, Church Street summoned James Schofield, butcher for assault, wilful damage, and refusing to quit, and Ann Schofield for refusing to quit. Mr Hodgson appeared for Wilson and Mr Sutcliffe was for the defence. The case against Mrs Schofield was first gone into, the evidence being to the effect that the previous Friday night a disturbance was taking place in the White Hart Hotel. Defendant was very unruly and declined to leave when requested both by the landlord and PC Blackburn, who however put her out. The case against the male defendant was to the effect that he created the disturbance in the complainant's house by taking up some ale that belonged to a soldier, and offering it to another member of the company. The landlord interfered and the defendant assaulted him, and a struggle between the two ensued, in which the defendant fell against the fireplace, damaging it and inflicting wounds upon his head from which the blood flowed freely... Mayor announced that they had decided to dismiss the case against Mrs Schofield, and also the charges of wilful damage against her husband, and he was fined 20s and costs for refusing to quit.

White Horse Hotel, 81 St James's Street, closed in 1965

Richard Hartley was serving the ale at the White Horse in 1824, and the house was a free house in 1888 and owned by John Butterworth. This was another hostelry that began life as a farm, at an approximate date of 1657. John Hargreaves (1657-1685), kept the inn, but also worked as a cooper. It was here in 1760, when George III became King, that 19s 4d was spent on ale, and later another 4s 'for more ale'. By the mid-1800s it was regarded as one of the premier taverns

The White Horse on St James's Street began life as a farm around 1657. (Briercliffe Society)

and served as a meeting place for many important gatherings. In 1861, the house was also home to Thomas Ogden and his wife Elizabeth, George Chester Ogden, who would later become long-time landlord of the Thorn Hotel, was also here, aged seventeen years, the son of Thomas and Elizabeth. Thomas Ogden was still the landlord at the White Horse in 1881, although he was then widowed. The White Horse was rebuilt several times, but its location remained very much the same. The hotel was referred to as the 'Big' White Horse, to avoid confusion with the 'Little' or New White Horse on Hammerton Street. On 20 March 1875, the *Burnley Gazette* reports that:

> A young man named Medcalf was charged with wilful damage caused on Thursday night at the White Horse Inn, St James's Street by the breaking of a number of glasses, the property of Thomas Ogden. He was ordered to pay 2s – the amount of damage caused, and fined 5s and costs in default seven days in prison.

The White Lion was another of those Burnley Inns which developed from a farm – the building we see today was built in 1910.

White Lion Hotel, 22 St James's Street

This is an old hostelry, for we know that William Spencer was serving the ale in the White Lion in 1824, and was still there in 1834. The White Lion actually developed from a farm with a stable, shippon and an acre of land known as White Lion Croft, with a butcher's shop adjoining. It was also an important coaching house in the nineteenth century, with coaches to Skipton and Colne departing from its yard on Sundays at twelve noon, Mondays at 5 p.m. and Wednesdays at 5 p.m. and 8 p.m. The White Lion is the symbol of Edward IV (1442-1483). Many 'lion' inns are said to date from this period in time. An early landlord at the White Lion was Robert Parker, who, it is believed, gave the narrow, garden-fronted lane behind his house its name – Parker Lane, as it is known today. The White Lion was offered for sale by auction on 28 August 1851 at the Swan Inn and described as:

> Lot 3: All that messuage inn or public house called the White Lion Inn with the tap house and small shop adjoining Parker Lane, yard and frontage (being corner premises) adjoining Saint James' Street and Parker Lane in Burnley. Tenant, Henry Whittaker's representatives.

The Wood Top Inn (or should it be 'Woodtop' as we see on today's inn sign?) has been extensively renovated at the time of writing.

The White Lion we see today was built in 1910, with an attractive cupola on the corner, oft missed during the hustle and bustle of modern life. The pub is also mentioned in the *Burnley Express*, 28 January 1882:

> Catherine Hopkins was summoned for assaulting Catherine Salmon. Mr J. Sutcliffe appeared for the complainant and said that both parties were married women, the complainant living on Parker Lane, and the defendant on Brook Street. On the evening of the 16th, the complainant went into the White Lion public house with a woman named Pickles and there found Hopkins, who objected to them being served, saying that she was the landlady. Pickles and Salmon afterwards left, and while the latter was standing at the former's door, defendant came up saying to Salmon that she would 'have her life, and would hang on the doorstep for it in the morning'. Complainant was called and bore out the statement, saying that she was a stall-keeper in the market, and that she was in fear of her life because of the defendant, as she had threatened to take her life before the winter was over. The Bench imposed a fine of 10 shillings and costs.

This is the old Woodman Inn when the landlady was Sarah Ellen Cronshaw, just before it was demolished and rebuilt around 1914. (Briercliffe Society)

Wood Top Inn*, 197 Accrington Road, reopened at time of writing (2007) following closure for a number of years

This was originally a beerhouse, for which a 'new license' was granted to a Mr Schofield in 1856. The inn was run by William Aspden in 1868 and by Nancy Aspden and Mrs Mary Aspden in 1879. Back in the 1880s, the Wood Top Inn was owned by W. and T. Taylor, a firm of Accrington brewers. The only other pub owned by this brewery company was the General Campbell. On 21 March 1868, the *Burnley Advertiser*, reports:

Breach of the Beer Act. William Aspden was summoned for a breach of this Act. PC Wilkinson said that the defendant was a beerhouse-keeper at Wood Top, and kept the Wood Top Inn. About half past seven o'clock on Friday the 7th inst., he visited the house. At one end of the table, there were some men playing dominoes, and at the other end they were playing cards. Witness said 'you are very busy' and the landlord replied, 'they are only playing for a glass of beer'. The defendant did not appear, but his wife when asked, had nothing to say. There had been no previous complaint against the house. The Bench said, on account of the good character of the house, they would only fine the defendant 5s and costs.

The old Yorkshire Hotel before it was rebuilt when the landlord was John Driver; this picture probably dates from 1896 when John was listed as landlord in the directories. (Briercliffe Society)

Woodman Inn, 127 Todmorden Road

The building we see today was built around 1914, by Fernande's Old Brewery, replacing a much older building a little way down Todmorden Road. The original inn was incorporated in a block of five cottages built by a man named James Briggs around 1818. James Briggs occupied the middle cottage in the block, and in 1838, began to sell beer. The cottage later became a beer shop under the name of the Woodman's Inn. A short time after this, James Bridge took in two more of the cottages and raised the roof, adding a third storey. A full license was then obtained, and later, the rest of the cottages were taken in. There can be no doubt as to the origin of the inn's name; Burnley Wood in the early 1800s really was a wood and part of the Towneley Estate. The Woodman was the first public house in that part of Burnley.

In the late 1860s, a Mr Thorpe became landlord of the inn; he used to live a short distance down the road in Woodman Square, next to an adjoining joiner's shop. This building had a datestone 'J.W. 1832' (Jeremiah Whittaker, 1832). An inn sign painted in the 1880s by a local artist named Ingham showed William E. Gladstone, the liberal statesman as a woodman. Subsequent landlords at the old inn, before it was demolished and replaced by the present building, included James Chaffer, from 1868 to 1879. Later came the Cronshaws, John Thomas and lastly, Sarah Ellen. Sarah Ellen was the last landlady in the old pub before demolition. An adjoining block of cottages, built by a man named Dean near the old Woodman Inn, was also pulled down at the same time as the old Woodman in 1914.

The Yorkshire Hotel was later rebuilt in an imposing style and must have been one of the grandest buildings in Burnley until it was demolished to make way for the Keirby roundabout. (Briercliffe Society)

Yorkshire Hotel, Yorkshire Street, closed in 1958

The site of the Yorkshire Hotel is an ancient one, and was originally occupied by the New House, with a triangular garden, kitchen, a flower garden and orchard situated at the rear of the building. A Captain Halstead, whose apparent claim to fame was that he was the last man in the town to wear a periwig, occupied it in those early days. Later a Mr Tattersall lived there, and following his death the premises were taken over by the army as accommodation for officers. From this billet, James Yorke Scarlett, a young captain in the 5th Dragoons, made the short journey to St Peter's church in December 1835, to marry Charlotte Anne Hargreaves, the daughter of Colonel John Hargreaves, owner of the local colliery and of Ormerod House. In getting wed to Captain Scarlett, Miss Hargreaves became Charlotte Scarlett! Captain Scarlett, of course, eventually became General Sir James Yorke Scarlett; he distinguished himself as our local hero during the Crimean War.

The previous Yorkshire Hotel.

In 1856, the house was that of T. Sutcliffe, of the Yorkshire Hotel, who also advertised for hire, 'two saddle horses, car and drag, and a horse and cart for removals at the shortest notice'. Richard Boys, the famed Burnley horse-drawn coach driver was the landlord in the early 1860s, as can be seen from the following article, taken from the *Burnley Advertiser*, 9 July 1864:

> Richard Boys of the Yorkshire Hotel was summoned for breach of the Beer Act. PC Lowe stated that on Sunday the 26th inst. at twenty minutes past seven in the forenoon, he visited the house and found two men that he knew, and who were not travellers with two glasses before them – one of whiskey, and one of rum. The defendant said that he knew nothing of it, as he was at church at the time. They were two friends of his who had called to see if he would take a walk, as was their custom. They had only just come in when the PC caught them. Fined 10s and costs.

On 1 February 1868, the *Burnley Advertiser* reports another incident involving the landlord of the hotel:

> Robert Harrison, landlord of the Yorkshire Hotel was summoned for a breach of the Beer Act. PC Cross stated that at forty minutes past twelve o'clock on the morning of the 20th inst., he saw a man come out of the tap attached to the hotel with a stone bottle containing ale, and another bottle in his pocket with rum or some other spirit in it. Defendant said that he knew nothing about it, he let the tap off. Fined 10s and costs.

The house was rebuilt in somewhat distinguished style, and in 1958, its license was surrendered to make way for the Keirby roundabout, although the building was not demolished until around 1960.